The Winning Parent

A Parent's Guide for the Journey of Competitive Sport

A System for Winning Now and Forever with your Children in Sport

By Daniel Massaro

Edited by Anthony W. Annunziata Ph.D.

Mairs & Shaw Publishing
New York

The Winning Parent

Massaro, Daniel

The Winning Parent

ISBN-13:9780692595374
ISBN-10:0692595376

Mairs & Shaw Publishing
Saugerties, New York

www.mairsandshaw.com

The 'Winning Parent' Resources:

 **@winningparent**

www.thewinningparent.com

Cover illustrations and artwork by Mary Beth Monterosso-Harris

Contents

About the Author

Founder of the 'Winning Parent' concept, Danny Massaro (pictured far left) has provided training and one to one coaching to hundreds of parents of competitive sports performers. He has also provided extensive support for coaches in the area of **parental relationships** through seminars and personal mentoring.

Danny has been a Lecturer of Sports Coaching for 20 years. Throughout the last decade, he has taught at the University of Central Lancashire where he has mainly lectured on Master's Program Modules in Coaching Philosophy, Coaching Processes, and Performance Psychology. He currently teaches on the ground breaking Elite Coaching Practice Level 4 Course that runs in conjunction with UK Sport and University of Central Lancashire, and whose participants are professional coaches employed by National Governing Bodies of Sport. In his time at the university Danny has won Awards for 'Innovation in teaching', and in 2013 he was awarded the 'We Heart You' special appreciation award direct from the University's Students Union.

Danny has coached and mentored his wife since she became a professional squash player in 2002. In 2014, Laura became Women's World Champion and became the only British woman in history to hold both The World Open and coveted British Open titles. In 2015, she won the U.S Open Championship for the second time and attained *World Number One* status. He has coached many other professional squash players too, with particular emphasis on the psychological support, and he continues to develop hundreds of younger players, some of whom have won National Championships and represented England. Danny has travelled the globe with his wife to all the major professional tournaments over the past eight years, thus experiencing rich understandings of different cultures and working under competitive pressure. Aside from the squash, Danny has supported many young professional performers with their psychological needs in soccer, swimming, boxing, ice skating, tennis, and athletics. Danny has recently had a chapter on the 'Art and Science of Coaching' published, where he gives his fascinating advice on coaching relationships, emotional intelligence, and how to involve sports science most effectively.

The Supporting Cast

Bryan Jones

Bryan has been lecturing in higher education since 1994 in sports psychology and sports coaching. He has worked with many professional sports performers and teams as a sport psychologist and strength and conditioning coach for the past 15 years. He is a mentor to several elite coaches throughout the country and has worked for and behalf of UK Sport, the Professional Footballers' Association, the British Olympic Association and the Rugby Football League. He is currently the Course Director for the first cross sport UKCC Level 4 elite coaching course which operates within The International Coaching and Performance Institute, at The University of Central Lancashire, England.

Dr. Ian Horsley

Ian has been a physiotherapist for over twenty years dealing with the full spectrum of sport performers from school level through working at the 2012 Olympic Games. Alongside running his own clinic, Ian has been a physiotherapist for England Rugby Union for 14 years, spending the last six years working with the Elite Playing Squad. Highly respected by those he treats, Ian is also the Lead Physiotherapist in the North West of England for the English Institute of Sport where he treats and advises many young performers (and their families!). Ian has dealt with many budding young stars and has excellent insight into the parent-child relationship and how it affects the process of recovery and injury prevention. Having worked with many world-class winners, Ian has gathered some great insight into what he believes makes for a healthy and successful way to be a sports parent.

David Pearson

David (a.k.a. 'DP'), pictured here with his daughter Jenny Duncalf *(a former world number two squash player)*, has been a coach for 35 years. He is a father of four: two daughters and two sons. David was the longest serving Head National Coach across all sports in the United Kingdom from 1995 until 2010. David has coached four World Champion squash players: two women and two men – coincidence!? Widely acknowledged as one of the best squash coaches in the world, DP continues to coach all players across the playing standard spectrum and from all corners of the globe. Winner of UK Sports 'Mussabini Medal' for outstanding coaching in 2000, DP is renowned for two special coaching skills.

First, his technical knowledge and ability to get his players to actually learn and apply new technical skills; and second, his ability to form strong and lasting relationships with players by focusing as much on the 'person' before him as on the player aspect of their make-up. The huge volume of young players he has seen come and go in his 35 year journey gives him a unique insight into aspects he feels have made the difference to those who have done well in sport but more important than that, have enjoyed happy and fulfilled lives. He remains a life coach to many people who have been lucky to experience his tutelage, mentorship, and friendship.

Basma Hassan El Shorbagy

Basma, a Civil Engineer by trade, is the mother of two boys Mohamed and Marwan who have both become world class sportsmen. Mohamed is currently ranked the world's number one player with Marwan not far behind. Both became World Junior Champions, both have graduated from university with degrees, and both are very rounded young men.

The main reason I wanted to interview Basma and introduce her to you in this book is because I have been very aware of how much her sons love her and include her in their individual careers. Mohamed in particular publically acknowledges the importance of his mother and requests that she follow him all over the world in his mission to become the best player on the planet. Mohamed said: *"She is the strongest person I have ever met in my life. No one can imagine the amount of pressure and work she has to take care of and to handle everything for me off court so I can perform the way I do on court!"* I was intrigued by this and decided to ask Basma if she would reveal some of her experiences, opinions, and strategies around her 'Winning Parent' philosophy. Thankfully, she agreed to talk to me, and over a four hour discussion at Starbucks in New York City, Basma revealed some fascinating insights.

John Trower

John has been involved in sport all of his life, and his reflections below acknowledge that. Interestingly, John has attended every Major Track & Field Championship since 1990, including five Olympic Games, eight World Championships, five European Championships and five Commonwealth Games either as a personal coach, TV commentator, or part of the Great Britain Team Management. A father himself, John has been an outstanding character in sports coaching and business for the majority of his professional life. Winner of UK Sport Coach of the Year in 1990 and 1992 for his work with three-time javelin world record holder Steve Backley OBE, John became Deputy Team Leader for the Great Britain Athletics Team at the Beijing Olympics 2008, and Team Leader with the very successful GB U23 Team in 2009. Currently, through work with Sports Coach UK and the University of Central Lancashire, John is mentoring coaches up and down the length of Britain as they aim to qualify as Level 4 Elite coaches in their respective fields.

Scott Fitzgerald

Aged 24, Scott (pictured here with his father) became the Welterweight Gold Medal winner of 2014 Commonwealth Games in Glasgow, Scotland. This was an amazing success for Scott as primarily he trained as a soccer player growing up as part of Blackpool FC's Academy. Coached by his father, who himself is a former amateur boxer, Scott took the longer and quiet route to the top, taking his time and staying out of the 'limelight' during his early stages of development, something which he feels helped him significantly. This year Scott has turned professional in the Light Middleweight Division and has continued with his father as his main coach.

Lauren Quigley

Lauren, aged 20, is an English competitive swimmer who has represented Great Britain at the FINA World Championships and England in the Commonwealth Games. She competed primarily in backstroke and freestyle events.

At the 2014 Commonwealth Games in Glasgow, she won three silver medals: 50m backstroke, 4x100m freestyle relay, and 4x100m medley relay. Lauren's mother also competed internationally as a swimmer and this has been brilliant for Lauren, yet at times it has also brought its own challenges.

Adam Henley

Adam, aged 21, (pictured right alongside Raheem Sterling) is an American-British professional soccer player who plays as a defender for Blackburn Rovers FC and Wales. Adam made his English Premier League debut in 2011 aged 17 showing incredible maturity as he played in a win against Manchester United at Old Trafford. Adam was part of the Wales National team who qualified for the 2016 European Championships for the first time in decades. Adam's parents have supported him every step of the way, and he credits them with his early maturity and ability to 'keep his feet on the ground' when growing up in the demandingly competitive environment of a professional football academy.

Laura Massaro (The wife!)

Laura has had an incredible career in professional squash. A professional player since 2002, Laura had previously represented England at every age group and won every National title to be won as a youth player. Professionally, Laura is the only English female player ever to win both the World Championships and the coveted British Open (the Wimbledon of squash). Winner of the prestigious U.S Open in 2011 and 2015, twice World player of the year, and Captain of England who are the current world champions.

Laura attained World Number One status in 2015. Her father was a strong influence growing up and was a major inspiration in developing Laura's two outstanding qualities that she is known and admired for: professionalism and mental toughness.

Foreword

I first met Danny when he attended one of my Neuro Linguistic Programming (NLP) programs. I was immediately struck by his enthusiasm and his willingness to embrace new concepts and ideas. Over the next couple of years, more than any other student, he used the tools and techniques he was learning in his teaching, in his coaching, and in his support of parents. In subsequent years, his skills expanded as he integrated NLP, the Graves Model, the Enneagram Personality System, and Ken Wilber's Integral Model into a coherent model of sports coaching. Not one to rest on his laurels, he was quick to realize that he also needed to work with his students' parents if the team was to achieve the best results. I know this gave him an extra edge and I sensed at the time he was rare amongst other sports coaches.

Danny and I joined to work together as part of Laura's team as we realized that in addition to working at a physical level, she also needed to work at a psychological level too. 'The difference that makes the difference' is often a result of working with the interior world as well as the exterior world, and this was true as Laura shifted from Number Ten in the world to World Champion.

In this revolutionary book, Danny shares all of his knowledge, skills, and expertise in this arena to help parents become 'Winning Parents'. The 'winning flightpath' he has designed is exemplary and makes it easy for parents to follow and act upon the many useful ideas included within. Packed as it is with practical suggestions, relevant research, and first-hand accounts from a rich array of winners, I urge you to delve in. As far as I am aware, this is the first book of its kind and will be of enormous use to any parent with children playing sports; it is also an amazing read!

Peter McNab

Peter McNab is an INLPTA Master Trainer, Vice President of the International Enneagram Association, and Founder Member of Ken Wilber's Integral Institute. He is also the author of: <u>Towards an Integral Vision: Using NLP and Ken Wilber's AQAL Model to Enhance Communication.</u>

Acknowledgements

I have to thank all those who have contributed so much to this book; especially those people who shared their expertise and experiences with me through interviews: Bryan Jones, Dr. Ian Horsley, David Pearson, Basma El Shorbagy, John Trower, Scott Fitzgerald, Lauren Quigley, and Adam Henley.

I would like to thank Paul Mairs and Richard Shaw for their commitment, hard work, enthusiasm, and unique insight. They gave me a massive lift just at the necessary moment, and provided a pathway for me to make this book come to reality. Their confidence in me and my material really did make a huge difference to the message, and their input and ideas brought everything to a higher level.

I would also like to thank Professor Anthony W. Annunziata for his tireless work in editing page after page of content. As well as clearing up much Anglo-American confusion, you made my writing style look much better than it really is! I would also like to thank Mary Beth Monterosso-Harris for her fantastic illustration work. You have captured the sentiment of my messages, and made the book considerably more appealing from a visual perspective.

Thank you to all the authors of all the books I have read in the past 20 years, especially Timothy Gallwey, Eckhart Tolle, and Ken Wilber. I may have never met any of you, but your support and wisdom has inspired and seen me through.

To those I have taught and coached: I would like to thank you for allowing me into your thoughts and dreams. In my view, coaching is the best job in the world, and it has been through our interactions, our struggles, and our successes that have given me so much experience to draw upon, much of which underpins this book.

Thank you Mother and Father. You brought me up at a young age, and in a time where advice and support was scarce. Your faith in me has never dwindled, and both of you feature heavily in this work; though you may not directly see it.

Finally, thank you my wife, Laura. Without you this book would not exist. What you have achieved in your profession is beyond inspirational. You have pushed me on, supported me, and most important of all you are the one person who always believes in me and my ambitions. Where others have doubted me, you have encouraged me, where others have laughed behind my back you have been honest to my face; and where others have crumbled away, you have been my rock!

In my opinion, Danny's enthusiasm, total dedication, and quest for knowledge in improving the whole athlete is totally unique. He inspires by example, brilliantly combining the roles of coach, mentor, and friend.

My two sons have both been lucky enough to have enjoyed and learnt from his inspiring coaching sessions, while also being encouraged to challenge themselves as far as they wanted to go. As parents, Danny always included us in any decisions regarding our son's development, while listening to our views with respect and empathy.

Our two boys both played for their county team before heading off to pursue their academic interests. Our eldest son became Captain and President of the squash club at Newcastle University, and our youngest son is now playing squash and studying at Harvard University, after playing at the International level, where he represented England at both the World and European Squash Championships.

Jacqui Smith

I first met Danny over a decade ago when he was my lecturer at university. From the moment I met him, it was abundantly clear he was a person with unique qualities; and I don't say this lightly.

Throughout years of involvement in the academic world and youth development, I have encountered some truly wonderful people. However, there is absolutely no question that Danny has resonated with my beliefs, values, and overall outlook to life. Only a select few people have ever had this type of powerful impact.

This book has been crafted in Danny's inimitable style. It is from the heart and empathizes with your distinct personal situation. It will undoubtedly have a profound impact on each and every reader.

Paul Mairs
Co-author of Coaching Outside the Box

Prologue

2010 - Getting it very wrong!

"You blew it even before you went on today. I could tell even before the match. That's why you played bad. That's why you lost."

"No I didn't I felt fine, it's you reading into it too much. I was fine."

"Come off it Laura, you were quiet all day and moody. You weren't excited enough to play."

"No I was fine, you don't know what it's like out there; you don't understand. I don't mean to play bad; do you think I want to? I don't want to let you down, I don't want to let myself down. It's causing me pressure."

"I am not causing you pressure; you **want** me to be here. I could be off doing something else. Don't put that onto me."

"I know, but I just don't want to lose. It means we have wasted money and your time to come here, and I know how 'gutted' you are when I lose, like now."

"It's the World Championships! Of course I am gutted! You've just lost, what do you expect me to be, happy?"

"No, of course not, just some understanding or a bit of sympathy or something, since you're my husband."

"Well it's just not in my nature, this is business. Besides, why can't you just see me as inspiration? I can't believe you see me as **pressure** when all I am trying to do is help you? You need to sort your head out, you're just soft and if you carry on being soft you will end up getting worse and worse until you hate playing! I know, I will stop coming. If I am so bad, I will stop coming; will that satisfy you?"

This wasn't so much an argument, but a one-way assault really: Accusations, threats, and various negative predictions of her future professional life. It makes me cringe to recall this particular argument because it was so one sided, and looking back now it is clear to see I was a big part of the problem, if indeed there was a problem at all. I continued the attack throughout the evening, but the low point came later while eating dinner:

"Why are you crying? This is what I was talking about: You've gone soft."

"Just leave me alone Danny. Just leave it, it's making it worse, just stop..."

We went to bed that night barely speaking.

Sound like a familiar tale? I hope not too familiar.

We were in Sharm el-Sheikh, Egypt for the 2010 World Squash Championships. A lovely place, a stunning hotel, and days full of sunshine. Somehow the emotion of sport had taken over me and my usual perspective had been lost. Slowly however, during the next day and as the emotions subsided, I had plenty of free time to reflect. My thoughts relaxed, and although I still believed in my 'accusations', I began to think I had best apologise; after all this was my wife and we needed to speak. Fortunately, I was coaching a highly ranked male squash player at the time and I trusted his opinions on professional squash and personal relationships, seeing as he was engaged to one of the top female players.

I asked Jon, "Am I too Intense with Laura?"

"Yes, yes you are (He couldn't say it quickly enough). "When you coach me its fine to be straight talking and go for a reaction from me. You're my coach and I know it isn't personal. You can say things that need to be said, even if I don't like them. With your wife, you just can't be so brutal. Not when she has lost, she needs to know you are there for her. It's the same with parents and their kids."

The guilt cloud started to form over me.

"It's not your job to make her play well or win. That is her job, you're here as a husband to support her through the good times and the bad."

Then, Jon said something profound, something that changed my whole perspective and professional relationship with my wife forever.

"What would you feel like if Laura came with you to work every day and told you what you were doing wrong, and how every time you had a bad day it was your fault?"

This hit me like a bullet out of the blue. Like a bullet does when it hits glass, it shattered my thinking and left me in emotional pieces. Guilt turned to self-loathing and embarrassment, ashamed of my self-centeredness and stupidity. The realization (or 'waking up' as I now refer to that moment) put me into a deep state of worry. A worry that I could get things so wrong and out of perspective. What was I doing? How had I become so nasty and unsympathetic to my wife's needs? I loved her very much, yet I behaved like I didn't care for her. In those moments, all I saw was a player, not a person.

2014 - Better!

In 2014, Laura became the World Open Women's Squash Champion. This followed winning the other major title in squash a few months earlier, the prestigious British Open. **She is the only British woman ever to achieve this double**. It was a 20 year journey to the summit of her personal Mount Everest. For 12 of those years she had been a professional athlete and I had been by her side every step of the way. As she celebrated calmly on the court, I was off running round the huge indoor arena in Penang, Malaysia, repeatedly jumping into the air like a stranded fish trying to leap back into the water. Each time I landed on the floor, I felt a huge force bouncing me back up into the air again, as if the whole arena floor had turned into one huge trampoline. Each time I landed and my brain shouted "World Champion", I was airborne again. Feeling a little calmer, I made my way back to the all glass squash court just in time to meet a tearful Laura as she walked off. We embraced and I lifted her off her feet. A perfect moment that **she** so gracefully earned.

The Pressure of Love

I have tried to logically explain my reactions in Laura's moment of victory. Looking back I think it was pure relief coming out. A release of pent up energy in my system that I hadn't been aware of. Without realizing it at the time, I believe that due to my close involvement in my wife's life and due to the fact we have a deep love and bond, I think I felt a huge burden of responsibility. I had advised her on so many important decisions, coached her through so many sessions, given her so many harsh 'home truths', and witnessed her go through much struggle and commitment on this journey she is on. I had encouraged faith and optimism, which was hard to provide on occasions. I dared to believe in the type and depth of support I offered, despite much self-doubt and external criticism coming my way. Most of all though, it was my wife's consistent faith in me that was probably the most subconsciously overwhelming aspect. This has never diminished at any stage of proceedings. There is huge responsibility when somebody believes in you that much, when somebody needs you on a daily basis, even when they just need you to do absolutely nothing. It complicates matters further when you love that person closely; it takes on deeper significance, and it is the 'pressure of love'. Although very different than being a parent, some similarities do exist. I believe the 'pressure of love' exists in both scenarios, and what I have learned through pain and joy gives me huge empathy for other people. I want to help you too.

Introduction

Being a parent is hard, very hard. Add into the mix the 'pressure cooker' atmosphere often encountered in competitive youth sport, and it becomes super hard. My main purpose for writing this book is to help reduce that pressure for you as you travel through the turbulent yet rewarding journey of competitive sport. Parents, children, and coaches all influence each other enormously on this journey; and the contents of this book can help make those interactions supportive, lasting, and effective.

For years I have been asked by parents to produce something like a book or an educational guide to help them deal with their children in and around competitive sport environments. They say I have a tendency to view things from the parental perspective, and that I have helped them with problems they've encountered on the sports pathway. My belief is that almost all parents just want what's best for their kids, yet many (not all) often go about it in ineffective ways. Even the better ones can sometimes demonstrate inappropriate or damaging behaviors at sporting events, in spite of the fact they have intended to offer their loved ones support and positive energy.

Now I'm not looking for absolution
Forgiveness for the things I do
But before you come to any conclusions
Try walking in my shoes

You'll stumble in my footsteps
Keep the same appointments I kept
If you try walking in my shoes
If you try walking in my shoes [1]

Martin L. Gore

Personally, I have covered the whole range of usefulness over the years. I have an appreciation of what it feels like to get things completely wrong; to interfere and pressurize without meaning to. Yet I also know how to make a huge, positive impact during competition and into the long-term. Along with my marital-coach role, the 20 years of experiences I have acquired working as a sports teacher and coach have also affected me profoundly. Again, I have rarely worked with a parent or fellow coach who doesn't want the best for the child. I do not believe people set out to deliberately undermine and limit a child's potential. Nor do I believe they try to diminish their independence, or reduce their enjoyment of their sport. But this is what I observe happening all too regularly, particularly in the competitive youth sport arenas. It can be simple things they do: Sideline shouting, car journey lecturing, public dressing downs, obsessing over ranking status, constantly comparing their child's status with others, arguments with officials or other parents, mockery of "the others". But mainly it occurs in subtle ways that are so gradual and slight that no one really notices them at the time. Just as damaging is the hyping up and use of social media to make youngsters the family headline news. The inflation of importance is just as dangerous as the over interference. The well-versed phrase, **'They are living through their kids'**, has not come from nowhere!

Unfortunately, the slow erosion of a child's enthusiasm to take risks, be creative, and remain individual is often only noticed in reflection years later. Here is just one common interpretation I've heard as to why teenagers stop loving sports:

"Yeah, looking back, I stopped enjoying it, and it all got too intense with the coaching, training, and arguments. I felt like I was letting my parents down because I wasn't improving and getting the results. They had spent a fortune on me in time and money. It was all too much, so I quit really. I just let sport in general dwindle away and the injury thing came as a bit of a convenient way out if I'm honest about it now."

This is a sad version of events, yet all too common. Of course there are positive tales and many children do well 'in spite' of their deprived or turbulent upbringing. However, my aim here is to help you become more skilled at delivering to your children a better environment for them to thrive in sport.

Three phases of youth sport participation

Canadian Researcher Jean Côté proposed three phases of participation from early childhood into late adolescence. They are the **Sampling years, the Specialising years and the Investment years**. He based his 3-stage model on the responses provided by the families of elite athletes who had been successful on the pathway of youth sports.[2]

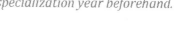

Côté's 3 phases of participation

SAMPLING YEARS	SPECIALIZING YEARS	INVESTMENT YEARS
6 -13 YRS. APPROX.	13-15 YRS. APPROX.	15 YRS. APPROX.
FUN	FOCUS ON 1 OR 2 SPORTS	SINGLE SPORT
PLAY EXPERIENCES	SPECIFIC SKILL DEVELOPMENT	COMMITMENT TO BECOME ELITE
ENCOURAGE EXCITEMENT	PRACTICE BEGINS	COMPETITIVE FOCUS
EXPERIMENTING	PLAY	INTENSE PRACTICE
INTERESTED IN MANY DIFFERENT TYPE SPORTS	FUN AND EXCITEMENT STILL IMPORTANT	TRAINING PROGRAMS
SPORTS LEADER COACHES	FINANCE & TIME COMMITMENTS	SETBACKS AND SACRIFICE
IDEAL PARENT RESPONSE	COACHING	**IDEAL PARENT RESPONSE**
ENCOURAGE EXPERIMENTATION	**IDEAL PARENT RESPONSE**	GREAT INTEREST AND SUPPORT
BE PLAYFUL WITH THEM	REMAIN FOCUSED ON PLAY AND ENJOYMENT	NON-SPORT SPECIFIC SUPPORT E.G. ORGANIZER, ADVISOR, SHOULDER TO CRY ON, LIFE ADVICE
ENCOURAGE OTHER ACTIVITIES	EMPHASIZE *SCHOOL* & *SPORT* ACHIEVEMENT TOGETHER	TREAT SIBLINGS AS INDIVIDUAL PEOPLE
SPOT THE GIFTS THEY MAY HAVE	GIVE FINANCIAL AND TIME COMMITMENT	SACRIFICES MADE IN TIME, SOCIAL EVENTS MISSED AND FUNDING
NON JUDGEMENT	DEVELOP A GROWING HEALTHY INTEREST IN THEIR SPORT	COMPANIONSHIP
PLAY AND ENJOYMENT IS PARAMOUNT		

Some sports require earlier investment years such as gymnastics and figure skating, but still experience at least three sampling years and one specialization year beforehand.

I asked Bryan Jones, from the University of Central Lancashire, to interpret Cote's findings:

Bryan: *Those parents involved at the 'sampling phase' see a sport as an opportunity for their children to play and have enjoyable experiences. They don't care what sport they choose to do as long as their children have fun. All the children in Côté's study tried out and enjoyed lots of sports before the age of 13, gaining an all-round perspective of sports before adolescence. This may include team games, individual sports, athletics, skill based games, or even gymnastic type sports. Usually from this, parents recognize their child has a 'gift' for one of the sports, and then if the child continues to want to perform in that sport, they tend to start specializing. This is from about age 13 to 15, and Côté found that it was crucial that play and enjoyment remained central elements, despite the youngster's practice and commitment increasing significantly. This is the* **'motivational climate'.** *The youngster needs to be specializing and committing time and effort to improvement and winning, yet the knack is for the parents and the coach to keep the attitude of 'challenging yet fun' with playfulness and practice well balanced.*

Where parents commonly go wrong in this **stage** *is when instead of focusing on the inherent enjoyment of playing and practicing sport, parents get caught up only in the* **winning** *at sport and throw all resources at it including their own time, money, coaching, equipment, analysis, and so on. So this starts to change the 'motivational climate' of the young player.*

Me: So they fast track to the last stage of investment too quickly?

Bryan: *Yes, that's it. They jump directly to the 'investment mindset' of more coaching, more competition, and focusing on just one sport too early. This is a crucial point because competition changes everything and it's this point that the* **family values** *are set in the youngster. If parents go too far down this road, they begin to treat their children as an* **asset** *and not just a young person.*

Me: So it becomes a means to an end, a way up the social ladder, or the way to obtaining a scholarship?

Bryan: *Exactly. The child feels this and if the parents are particularly forceful and anxious, it gets really damaging in terms of the motivational climate of that family and particularly within that child.*

From being babies, children learn to get attention by conforming to social norms that are seen as valuable and set down by the tribe. If they see that their parent's

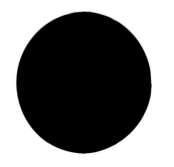

evian.

Pure by Nature from the French Alps

Satisfy Your
Thirst

Purchase evian® Natural Spring Water
and other refreshments here. We'll conveniently add
them to your SeaPass account and your Mini Bar will
be replenished throughout your voyage.

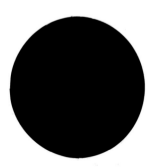

emotions are only positive when they win, yet negative when they lose or have a bad day, then clearly they are affected deeply. Pressure begins to rise and enjoyment slowly diminishes if winning isn't achieved because the youngster feels like they are 'letting the tribe down'! Kids can deal with disappointments for themselves, but it is much more damaging when they feel they are letting the family down, and this is when the enjoyment wanes away. We cry for recognition most of our lives because some of our biggest fears are to be alone, unworthy, and unrecognized. As we move into our teenage years it is ever more important to be recognized by our social network as we aim to establish our identity and sense of status.

Me: This reminds me of a quote from Louis Zamperini, the man who is a prisoner of war survivor and former Olympic distance runner, whose life story was made into the movie 'Unbroken'. He said: "I've had many years to wonder why as a child I caused so much mischief, and I've come to the conclusion that what I really wanted was recognition. That's not the same as attention. Attention comes and goes, usually quickly. Recognition lasts longer. I wanted to be admired. At first my running got me noticed; with repeated improvement and a go all out attitude, notice became recognition."[3]

Bryan: *Yes, exactly. Give them recognition for effort and improvement. Notice more elements where they impress you. Those parents who have the wisdom to give their children space and to hold onto the notions of play, fun, and learning, while positively supporting their practical needs, have been shown to create many short and long-term psychological and social benefits for the child.*

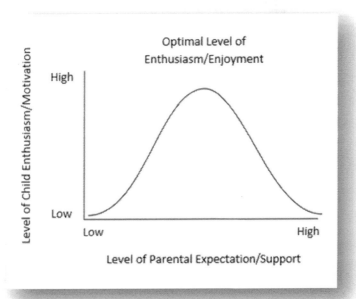

In most cases enjoyment and enthusiasm to compete remain; while long-term characteristics such as resilience, social empathy, self-determination, and optimism begin to develop. The key is to find that intermediate level of expectation and support. This can be illustrated in the simple inverted 'U' type graph that follows. High and low expectations often result in the lowering of enthusiasm from children over time, whereas intermediate involvement yields the healthiest results.

Côté admits that his findings are an incomplete picture of all families, all over the world through all of time, but the stage models are a good start and provide flexibility for people. In this case Côté suggests, "The role of parents changed from a leadership role in the sampling years by getting children to try many sports, to a committed supporter in the specializing years, to a to a follower/supporter role in the investment years."[4]

Most crucially Côté pointed out that in all the families studied:

A: Parents did not put any kind of pressure on the child regarding the type of sport they should specialize in.

B: Parents responded to each stage appropriately by fostering optimal learning environments, rather than creating new demands or pressure.

I have considered all three phases in this book and as you read on you will learn how applying the stages of the 'Winning Flightpath' can help you be at your best during each phase.

Three Perspectives: The Parent – The Child – The Coach

The fascinating thing about competitive youth sport these days is that children work with more coaches than ever before. Coaching has been built up as a big and lucrative industry, especially in the past 10 years. It is not necessarily a positive or negative thing in terms of helping parents, but what is certain is that coaches and trainers are here to stay. The way you all relate to each other is important, and speaking as a coach I certainly appreciate those parents who facilitate the process rather than hinder it.

Instead of just giving one perspective of this threesome, below I have presented the typical questions and concerns that each might have. By thinking of each other's perspective we can understand more about the possible blocks to good communication, ways of enhancing trust and strong teamwork.

Problems, Questions, and a Solution

Here are the typical problems or questions sports parents have:

- Why does watching my child compete cause so much emotion to rise to the surface?
- How can I control myself better when I watch my son/daughter play?
- Why won't my child listen to me when all I am trying to do is help them?
- Why do I get so upset when they lose, yet so happy when they win?
- My husband/wife thinks they are a coach all of a sudden, how can I get them to back off without hurting their feelings?
- Can I learn anything that will help me cope with the competitive development of my child?
- We are spending so much time and money on them, yet they aren't trying hard enough! What should we do?
- Can you help me view my child as a winner no matter what the scoreboard says?
- The coach wants them to up their training and stop playing other sports as much. What should we be doing?
- I think my son/daughter is too obsessed with their sport, how can I get them to calm down and be more rounded?
- How can I handle myself better when I think my child has played poorly, not tried and lost?
- How can I handle myself better when I think my child has played brilliantly, tried their best and lost?
- How can I handle myself better when I think my child has played poorly, and not tried but yet won?
- How can I handle myself better when I think my child has played average and won?
- How can I help make my child really learn that all they can do is their best, as they can`t control external factors?
- My child has been selected for the next level up on a regional or national team; what is the best way to react?
- I fuss over my child's sport a lot and I know I am doing it; how can I reduce it?
- I am too critical of my son/daughter, and know I am when I do it, how can I reduce it?
- I can't watch my child play because it is too stressful. How can I enjoy the experience instead of dreading it?

- How much should I trust coaches?
- How much coaching is the correct amount?
- How can I tell if a coach has authentic long-term interests for my child's development and not just for their back pocket?
- What are the good qualities that I can look out for in coaches?
- Should I be noticing my child **competing** more often or **practicing** more of the time?
- Is it good for my child to specialise in one sport or play other sports as well? What are the issues with this?
- I can never tell, am I doing a good job as a sports parent?
- My kids are completely different; they react to the same thing in different ways. How can I deal with that?

Here are the questions and issues that coaches tend to ask when it comes to working with parents:

- How can I help set up shared values and philosophies with parents and players?
- What are the best ways to help parents understand their role in the development of their child's sports experience?
- How can I help reduce parental behavior that I understand to be at best limiting, at worst damaging?
- Is it my responsibility or duty to coach parents as part of the process of youth development?
- What should I do if I sense that parents are spoiling their kid's progress, but they don't know it?
- Are there any specific tools that a coach can develop in order to help deal with parents?
- Where can I learn more about the influence of the parent – child – coach relationship?
- I learned nothing about working with parents on my coaching courses. Who can help me deal with these delicate issues?

Here are the common questions and concerns sports children have with their parents:

- How can I help parents understand my feelings more?
- What things can I put effort into so that my parents will relax?
- How can I use my sports experience to enjoy my bond with my parents?

- What specifically is expected of me by my parents and coach? Are these the same?
- My parents support me in many ways, (equipment, money, transport, time, food). How can I let them know I really appreciate such support?
- Is there a way I can calmly talk to my parents about the pressure I sometimes feel?
- I want to take a break; how can I tell them?
- How can I put in lots of effort and be dedicated but still have a life as well?
- I don't want to be given attention for just my sport. How can I be loved for being me the person, not just me the athlete?
- When I perform poorly and lose interest, how can I talk to parents about it?
- How can I ask my parents to involve themselves more?
- How can I help my brothers/sisters with their interests, so all attention isn't just on me?
- How can I use my parents as inspiration to perform and train better?
- If my parents won't change and can't understand the pressure they put on me, how can I deal with it better?

A Solution 'The Winning Flightpath'

The solution to all of these questions are available. What I present to you in this book is a unique **7-stage process** that I believe will help you in respect to all of the questions and problems you may struggle with when it comes to being a sports parent. Each step provides clear practical ideas and helpful pointers of how you can be much more helpful to yourself and your family. I firmly believe these ideas will result in less stress, less nervousness, fewer arguments, lower cost of time and financial investment. When implemented, I believe they will lead to more enjoyment, more appreciation, and more winning too! Most other books, media coverage, and research to date are great at pointing out the mistakes and failings of parents, but by designing the **'Winning Flightpath'** I have given you a roadmap for improvement and success rather than generalised criticism. In this regard, I believe the format and content of this book is totally unique. The **Winning Flightpath** is easy to follow and with a little effort you can instantly soar to new heights of sports parenting.

In support of the **'Flightpath'** I have included research from science and perhaps most importantly from people who have been winners themselves as parents, businesspeople, and sports professionals.

Winning

Clearly, this book is about Winning. I called it 'The Winning Parent' after all. I did so purely to grab your attention because the word 'winning' usually does that to people. In our modern world, it is a clear fact that winning in sports is held as one of life's greatest accomplishments, and endless effort and emotion is spent trying to acquire it. Maybe it is 'not losing' that we want! Being a winner is so much better than being a loser isn't it? No matter what culture, what age, or what personality we are who doesn't love a winner, or being a winner? Unfortunately, you have been tricked slightly. You may have presumed that this book will help you win at some sort of competition. For example, by reading this book you may have assumed: "I will become the best sports parent of all the sports parents I know and my child will acknowledge that one day." Maybe you will even get more followers on Facebook and Twitter!

The truth is that this book is actually about relationship building, specifically parent-child relationships, and the relationship your child has with a sport itself. It is more about checking in on what is really important to you, your shared family philosophy. It is about building your own definition of 'winning' based on your own values and beliefs in life. This book is really about asking you to check whether or not you still want those values and beliefs to dominate your thinking, and about helping you to stick with those choices in your actual behavior.

For the time being you are the adult and ultimately you are captain of your children on this early part of their life's journey. It is up to you as parents with your children on board, to determine where you want to go on your family flight and how you want to pilot it! Whatever your perception of a 'Winning Parent' may be it will most certainly require clever piloting skills as you search for and navigate necessary risks and pressures. The question is can you Captain in such a way that your children survive, thrive, and eventually learn to become Captains for themselves and ultimately for others.

As these two proverbs point out:

"Ships in harbor are safe but that's not what ships are built for."[5]

And

"Smooth seas do not make skilful sailors."[6]

Using your Book

"The book to read is not the one that thinks for you but the one that makes you think."[7]

Harper Lee

This book has been designed for you to use it however you like. If you like information, there is plenty of it. If you like doing exercises and reflecting on personal scenarios then this book is for you! I believe the most effective way to use the book is as a personal diary and this is why I have left blank pages for you to make your own personal notes and scribbles.

The flightpath always requires you to apply your own unique situation to it, so in a way it is what you write and scribble that will have greatest real life impact on your family. Parents who have used the exercises so far have reported that it was most helpful to take the book along with them to tournaments, training, and competitions. It is a perfect time to read and remind yourself of some of the lessons you have taken from the information provided. Even just one glance at something you know really helps can change your whole experience.

- *The flightpath has been designed for you to use how you want to.*

- *You can even change the sequence if it fits your thinking better.*

- *It has been provided as a simple structure for you to put your own ideas into.*

- *Each stage has the potential to help you, but only if you apply it to your own personal situation.*

- *Like anything that is worth accomplishing, it requires effort to get the best from it.*

• *If it feels like too much effort, take a break before you get overwhelmed.*

• *It may be just one area of the flightpath that changes everything for you.*

• *Share it with your children. It can be great for conversation.*

"So when we look at reforming education and transforming it, it isn't like cloning a system. It's about customizing to your circumstances and personalizing education to the people you're actually teaching. And doing that, I think, is the answer to the future because it's not about scaling a new solution; it's about creating a movement in education in which people develop their own solutions, but with external support."[8]

Sir Ken Robinson

Elephant in the room!

Q. But you're not a parent yourself, why listen to you and the advice provided in this book?

A. If you believe the only people who can advise you on parental support are parents, then this book will undoubtedly change your perspective. Occupying a neutral position while working with young athletes and their parents allows me to see the bigger picture more clearly. From this position, I am not clouded by my own paternal fears and biases; enabling me to uphold an open minded and impartial outlook.

Additionally, I have been able to generate a huge sense of empathy for parents throughout my coaching experiences with my wife, which has been an incredible journey that has seen her become the **World's Number One female squash player**. As you will read in this book, her career has been full of ups and downs and it has been an emotional rollercoaster. The moments of displayed love, care, discipline, frustration, anger, sympathy, trust, and happiness mirror all the emotions parents encounter due to the deep love and ambitious drive connected with their child's sporting 'Flightpath'.

Finally, it's important to reiterate, the insights and advice articulated from all kinds of sources, including those of professional world champion athletes, world class coaches, and 'Winning Parents' provide some of the most astute, inspiring, and educational information parents could ever wish to receive!

Before you fly - Taking the pressure down

This chapter helps reduce the pressure that sports parents typically put onto themselves whether they feel it or not. As we feel less pressure, there will be a greater chance of our natural skill and love emerging. Chances are we will **flow** better with our children and this alone can work wonders. We will act the way we do around our best friend: Relaxed, natural and in the moment.

Your personal situation

> *"I am not going to treat you all the same. Giving you the same treatment does not make sense because you're all different. The good Lord, in all his infinite wisdom, did not make us all the same. Goodness gracious, if he had, the world would be a boring world, don't you think? You are different from each other in height, weight, background, intelligence, talent, and many other ways. For that reason each one of you deserves individual treatment that is best for you. It may take the form of gentle encouragement or it may be stronger. That depends on you."[9]*
>
> *John Wooden*

We all have very personal situations, especially when it comes to raising youngsters, with circumstances that are totally different from those of other parents and their children. Remember to utilize your own circumstances when considering topics in this book. For me, there is a lot of generalizing and parent bashing out there regarding what parents should and shouldn't do. Therefore, I have sympathy for many parents, as there are many misguided notions and agendas espoused by coaches to deal with, not to mention a plethora of choices for parents to make concerning the best club or training environment for their child. Even though lots of the information makes sense and is shielded in diplomatic words, the basic premise or subtext in lots of research and opinion on sports parenting goes like this:

> *"When you as a parent do 'X' and 'Y', it is bad for your child. So, instead DO what we suggest because we know better than you." AND...*
>
> *"If you don't do what we recommend, you are likely to remain an unfit parent who is most probably damaging your child's future." AND...*
>
> *"Just in case you have any doubts, here's some specifically chosen research that SUPPORTS my opinion. So I am right after all!"*

I have certainly done this myself, but as time has gone on I have realized my views have been too general and often inappropriate. In an attempt to feel certain and demonstrate my knowledge, I have simplified the complex nature of parenting and individual circumstances.

This can have a demotivating effect because there you are, trying your best, managing your situation with all the skill you can muster, yet suddenly you are made to feel as if you are typical of someone damaging their child. Not only is this disheartening, but it puts fear into you. I also believe it is unfair.

Your personal family situation, your culture, your economic means, your gender, your accommodation, your upbringing, your relationship status, and your individual children make your personal situation **highly unique**.

BE CAREFUL

Clearly, if a child is being mistreated then intervention is important. If a person witnesses a child being abused and reports this abuse as being wrong, this is not the situation as described before where a person thinks they "know better". They are taking this course of action as they are a thoughtful, caring individual who recognizes that this mistreated child is in a bad situation. No child should be in an environment where they are on the receiving end of mistreatment or abuse.

But back to the key point being addressed here. In sport terms: Where you live, the facilities available to you, the coaching traditions, the weather, the level of competition, the role models, choice of sports, media coverage, and local competition structures are all major ingredients in your personal situation. **So please remember: There is no BEST way, just an APPROPRIATE way for you.**

Uncertainty is your friend

"Let me ask you a question: Do you like surprises? If you answer "yes", you're kidding yourself! You like only the surprises you want. The ones you don't want you call problems! But you still need them to put some muscle in your life. You can't grow muscle—or character—unless you have something to push back against."[10]

Tony Robbins

There are no answers in this book that will make your sports journey with your child certain. I know it is hard to accept that because **being certain** things will work out well brings a sense of relaxation and calmness. A sense of certainty takes away the worry and the wondering. Maybe this is why so many fall prey to sports advertising in the way of equipment and gadgets that "will give you more power" or sports drinks that "will make you last longer!" Promises of certain results, if you buy our product!

We all like listening to the coach who promises to improve your child's sports performance if you commit to their guaranteed principles. This is something I have encountered many times over the years in youth sports, with coaches espousing assured statements such as *"I will GUARANTEE we will take your child to the next level"*, or *"playing with our club/organization will ASSURE they secure a college scholarship"*.

However, a paradox in life is that while we seek **CERTAINTY**, we must learn to both enjoy and accept it is an **UNCERTAIN** process. Our need to be certain also lowers our ability to take risks and put faith in our own resources.

Uncertainty lowers boredom and is why sport itself is exciting. Things remain fresh because we just do not know for certain how things will turn out. We can guess which course of action is best to take and use experience to help shape our futures, but we still have much uncertainty about how life will turn out. Anyone who believes that they can make certain that a child's future will turn out a specific way are in many ways deluded, or what's more likely is they harbor an ulterior motive.

Do you have a tendency to want to make too much certain when it comes to advising and helping your children in their sport? How would your life be if you already knew exactly everything that was going to happen? Would you wish to find out if you could? Maybe if you could travel into the future you would? But even if it was one filled with wonderful things, how long would your relief and joy last before they were replaced by boredom?

Does uncertainty bring some adventure to life? Is it time to celebrate the uncertainty? Rather than worrying about the future, and in this case how your children will turn out, accept and appreciate the uncertainty because in simple terms:

A) You are stuck with it!
B) It keeps life exciting!
C) You will relax much more and align yourself with how life really works!

Contradictions and paradoxes

"So I think we have to change metaphors. We have to go from what is essentially an industrial model of education, a manufacturing model, which is based on linearity and conformity and batching people. We have to move to a model that is based more on principles of agriculture. We have to recognize that human flourishing is not a mechanical process; it's an organic process. And you cannot predict the outcome of human development. All you can do, like a farmer, is create the conditions under which they will begin to flourish."[11]

Sir Ken Robinson

Shaping people is a process full of contradictions and paradoxes:

- *It is about things you can see as much as things you can't see.*

- *It is about changing as much as staying true to your roots.*

- *It is about patience as much as it is about urgency.*

- *It is about confident direct leadership and letting others lead.*

- *In sport, it is about winning while losing and losing while winning.*

- *The big picture and the small one, the long-term view and the short-term needs.*

- *Guesswork as much as facts; intuition versus intellect.*

- *The use of scientific support while relying on folklore and traditions.*

- *Good things growing from pain, and bad things growing from too much pleasure.*

Can you think back to an experience of yours that at the time you felt was awful for you; and yet now when you reflect on it, it played a vital role in your development?

Can you think back to a time when you took a risk and got away with it? Something you would never do now or admit to, especially to your children. Think how going through that experience shaped your life in a positive way.

Some people have a special ability when it comes to relating and inspiring children. That wonderful ability to find the right words to say just at the right time is as artistic as any painter's stroking a brushstroke in the appropriate place. Some people take to parenting much easier than others, but much depends on the particular child. Certain children are trickier to deal with and shape. Gender differences, personality differences, and changes in maturity all affect how a parent hits it off with a certain child. Some children are inspired more by their father, and some by their mother. Indeed we can see vastly different outcomes between siblings all coming from the same parental treatment.

So in many ways parents aren't in control of their children's ultimate destiny as much as they like to believe. While being vastly important, parents are not **solely** responsible for how their children turn out, particularly in sport. Life is chaotic and sport certainly is. However, parents can be educated on how they can treat kids differently based on their differences, such as their genetic makeup. John can be spoken to differently from Jane, rather than John and Jane being spoken to in exactly the same manner in order to achieve a more beneficial long-term developmental outcome.

Take the pressure off yourself a bit. Accept that contradictions and paradoxes need to play their part, as does luck. Put a focus on creating a way to trust each other, to share some understandings; and then you can simply be there for each other as life evolves. **Think of this gardening metaphor:**

- Nature x Nurture = Outcome.
- Roots nourished by parents.
- Life events just as influential as parenting.
- Like flowers, children need room.
- Each plant has its own needs.
- Organic better than forced.
- Parents can only do so much, weather dependent.

Can you add your own meaning of the previous metaphor? At least one below:

_____

_____

_____

_____

_____

Remembering their individuality

"They are all different. There is no formula. I could name players, all who were spirited (see above!) but in a different way. You can't work with them exactly the same way. You've got to study and analyze each individual and find out what makes them tick. I wish there was a formula. The same thing won't work with every team. It depends on the personnel. So you have to know the individuals you are working with."[12]

John Wooden

Think about the following questions:

- *What things make your child unique and who they are?*

- *Why are they special to you?*

- *What makes them unique in terms of the talents they have?*

- *Why do they amuse you?*

- *What are their particular fears?*

Playing styles

Children tend to approach sport in different ways and express themselves in different styles. Below are just 4 possibilities:

Hard workers: They make small improvements over the long term, they are dedicated, they want honest feedback, they constantly put in high levels of effort, they're able to think long-term, they are strong willed, and they know discipline pays off in the end.

Naturally gifted: The game seems to come easy, they make quick improvements, they display a variety of skills, they develop their own ideas, they experience short-term success *(especially during their formative years)*, they have flowing movements, and they display a high level of cognitive functioning skills (e.g. decision making, anticipation, and awareness etc.).

Structured Thinkers: They like a plan and information, they are logical in their thoughts, they like to engage in discussion, they play in and like patterns of play, they demonstrate a *"we can work it out"* approach, they build by design, and they have difficulty with being creative.

Unstructured Creative: They have random ideas, they're experimental, they try new skills and techniques, they are fun based, they like play and game-based practices, they find structure hard to stick with, and they are spontaneous.

Each player will have a natural way to approach trying to master a sports challenge. It is always helpful to appreciate the way a child views the sport so we can understand their natural motives for playing in the first place. Unfortunately, this point is often overlooked by many people involved in youth sport, leading to many youngsters feeling demotivated and not coming close to unlocking their true potential.

Without a player feeling motivated and energized, it is unlikely their journey through sport will ever be as good as it could have been. This is the case no matter what playing style they are. The key is identifying their way of thinking and their motivation for playing the sport. A rigid approach, or an outlook where 'one size fits all', will undoubtedly keep players limited.

The maturity in one's natural playing style is enhanced when players are conscious of their own strengths and are willing to adapt where necessary over the years. Additionally, the wise parent will understand the importance of matching the child's playing style with their personality and supporting their child accordingly because this is where deep motivation lives.

Understanding personality for sports competition

One thing that I hear constantly in professional sport is how everyone is different. Managers, coaches, and athletes talk a lot on the merits of **"being treated** as an individual", having **"good man management skills"**, and implementing **"individualized training programs."** Warnings are given about the dangers of taking away a player's unique style and of treating everybody too much the same way. If I could summarize all the best advice I have received from expert sport coaches, the main thrust of it would go something like this:

> *"The thing is, Danny, to be a great coach you've got to get to know the individual, what makes the individual tick. Also, the players need to know themselves too and how they operate best. There isn't just one way, you see. Everyone is different and you need to remember that most of all."*

One finds it hard to disagree with this, despite the reality of how much of a difficult mission these wise managers, coaches, and athletes have just set out. Additionally, these individuals also remind me of the following point:

> *"Oh Danny! Another thing that's vital: Make sure you always stick to your principles. Never compromise your values or change your philosophy because of player power. Yes, know yourself and always stay true to yourself; that is most crucial!"*

HELP!

Think of *three* or *four* top athletes of all time from a particular sport and you will easily distinguish differences in their style, approach to training, lifestyle, and preferences of coach and motives for participation.

Who is most like your child from your examples?

Why do you think you picked this athlete?

In what way does this athlete remind you of your child?

Of course they will have shared many winning habits regarding competitiveness, practice, and mental strength under pressure; but they will remain very individual and unique. Perish the thought that athletes become like robots being treated all the same, following all the same instructions and performing in identical patterns. We are all very different, and we all need to be considered on a totally individual basis. However, in saying that, it is important to understand that we do have similarities in relation to our character and behavior which allows us to categorize individuals into certain groups.

To now talk about categorizing personality seems a bit silly after what I have just written about everyone being individual. To propose that there are categories of personality seems quite limiting and contradictory to what I said about uniqueness of people (contradictions again!). It seems however that neuroscientists are finding more and more evidence that people do have certain patterns of personality ingrained into their brains through a combination of nature (genes) and nurture (our environment). Professor Dario Nardi, from the University of California, discovered that certain areas of the brain are extra active for people of certain personality types.[13] Nardi found, for example, that those known as creative personality type people were easy to predict just by looking at brain scans, and those who are ordered and disciplined equally easy to identify, thus at last bringing evidence to what psychologists have been predicting for some time. Personality habits exist within us from birth and grow stronger and more hardwired in our brains the more we repeat those habits. The posh word for this is what brain researchers call **"neuroplasticity"**. Like muscles in our body, regions of our brain grow the more they are used.

So now let us link the two ideas of sport and personality.

The word personality originally meant mask! The mask is what we show and act out to the world. It is something we use to hide behind as well as get things we want. One of our basic human needs is to be connected to people, and as soon as we are born our brain begins playing a range of wonderful tactics to get the attention of other people, so that we can connect with them. Any attention will do as long as we connect or get noticed. Examples the baby brain might use is smiling, crying, gesturing, silence, and eye contact. As we get older these may develop into tantrums, giving cuddles, performing, hiding (come and get me!), behaving well, being clever, helping, flattery, sulking etc.

Some psychologists have predicted that as we begin to get attention in particular ways in our childhood, we basically keep repeating the behaviors that work in getting attention and so certain areas of our brains get trained particularly hard. These areas then grow and basically start to become the default setting by which we use to connect with people as we grow through our childhood. This is how personality (the mask/act we use to get attention) is trained and ingrained. By the time we are teenagers, our personality pattern is thriving, and if we are not careful it becomes our only predictable way to connect with other humans. If sulking for attention has always worked, or winning things and being a little achiever has gotten noticed, then guess what? These well-trained behaviors are going to continue into adulthood! Of course, it is more complicated than this, but I hope you get the general point.

Types?

The earliest researchers proposed distinction between introvert and extrovert types, with psychologist Hans Eysenck being a prominent figure in this area. Those that are quiet, shy, and withdraw from people being of introvert type, while those who are loud, sociable, and expressive being of extrovert type. Susan Cain's excellent book <u>Quiet</u> delves into this area brilliantly.[14] Other systems of typing personality include the popular Myers-Briggs Type Indicator (MBTI)[15], where feelings, senses, and emotional aspects are included, along with introversion and extroversion. The system that I want to introduce to you is called the Enneagram.[16]

The Enneagram: One system of personality profiling

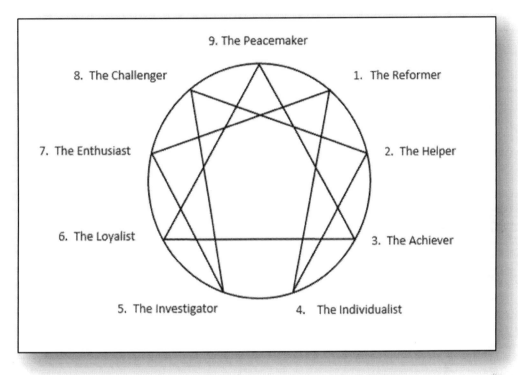

An ancient and dynamic shape, which comes from the Greek word 'ennea' and 'grammos' meaning nine-pointed figure. It was adapted to personality typing by Claudio Naranjo a noted Gestalt Psychologist.[17]

This system uses an ancient nine-pointed star shape to illustrate nine spaces of personality that are thought to exist. Thousands of people all across the world have enjoyed using the Enneagram for personal development, coaching, business leadership, and relationship improvement.

The Enneagram model of personality typing proposes that people hover in one of the nine spaces, while occasionally existing in other spaces, depending upon their stress levels and life situations. I really like this model because it is brave enough to suggest certain set patterns grow and exist in people, while allowing factors such as personal maturity and moment to moment situations to bring flexibility to the particular person. We all know that people have certain personality patterns, but we also know how different the same people can be at different times too.

The Enneagram system allows the best of both worlds. It provides a structure to discuss the personality patterns and habits of an individual, while understanding that two people who are of similar type may be totally different. Intuitively this makes common sense, rather than pigeonholing a person into one type. It makes people feel less boxed-in and more open to admit their typical patterns, while retaining a sense of individual being. It helps me as a coach to understand helpful and limiting patterns that people operate with, while also understanding how very individual that person is too.

Example:

8 space individuals are excellent at taking charge and fighting battles, especially when the going gets tough. So 8's can actually create confrontation to help themselves play better. The flip side for 8's (as there is with every number space), is that they get stuck when they over-analyze or think too much when things start to go wrong. Operating mainly from the gut, they feel weak and can malfunction by in effect moving into the 5 space, which is the 'information is king' space. They will suffer from too much internal chatter and can quite easily boil over into blind frustration and illegal aggression. So the tactic to use against the typical 8 personality is to slow them down so they have time to think, and keep quiet on the outside; be nice to them so there is no conflict, and maybe make fun of them in a nice way. They will lose the fire that they so depend on while becoming very self-critical and embarrassed. This is surely a much better way to play the strong dominant 8 type.

If however the particular type 8 in question has maturity and self-awareness concerning their '8' tendencies, they can put plans into place to counteract the possible problems that can arise. They can learn to embrace the aspects of themselves they like to trust and be aware that opponents might cleverly be trying to knock them out of their stride. This can be a wonderful advantage to have in the battle of mind games which certainly play a key part in competitive sport.

A fun platform for discussion

So the Enneagram system becomes a really useful structure that gets people reflecting and chatting about parts of themselves that normally they wouldn't consider opening up about. It is not easy to begin a discussion about one's own personality if one has nothing to build the conversation around. Quite often when I have asked people to describe their personality, they really struggle to put sentences together. People tend to know what they are not, much more than what they are! In fact, it's by the process of elimination of other suggested types that people begin to gain more insight into themselves. "*That's definitely not like me*", many will declare. Then, to support this premise they will continue to assert in an ambiguous fashion: "*Because I am someone who likes to worry, in a positive way, I am reliable you see and always double check that we prepare so nothing goes wrong. Others say I am too pessimistic but I don't feel like that. To me, it's those who are overly upbeat and never take anything seriously enough*". **Once we understand the box we are in, perhaps only then we can climb out of it to new heights.**

I have found using the Enneagram with sports people to be liberating as opposed to limiting. Currently, I work with some sports competitors who hover around type 1 personality, and despite similar key motivations and habits they remain very distinct from each other. Saying this, I still consider a person's level of maturity (values) the most important factor in professional success. Also, we have to consider cultural influences, specific situations, mood, health, socialization, and learning.

BE CAREFUL

A personality type is not an excuse for one's behaviors. We still have choices to make as individual and responsible people. We all have tendencies and urges to behave certain ways but learn to resist and compensate what we do, for most of the time at least! Bringing awareness to your personality space is meant to help you mature and develop not simply reduce yourself to a robot operated by forces outside of your control.

Idea: Individual personality test

Find a fun way to interact with your children around their personalities. Discover all your differences and the different ways you see the world. Do it with a light touch and involve yourself too. I recommend the Enneagram but I am sure you can find your own method too.

The genetic lottery

"Choose your parents carefully!"

A strong recent example of the need to consider individuality is the reference to genetics in David Epstein's award winning book <u>The Sports Gene</u>.[18] For much of the past ten years there has been a push towards 10,000 hours of practice being a bare minimum to reach peak performance no matter what is one's makeup.[19] It appears many coaches have accepted that the '10,000 rule' is sacrosanct across the board in all types of sports. But, suddenly, evidence suggests that number or indeed any set total, isn't as certain as previously populated; "there is no magic formula" as Epstein says.[20] Epstein brings powerful scientific arguments in relation to gender, race, willpower, age and physiology which again add complexity to the standard folklore that if you practice hard enough you can do anything. He uses science to reveal deeper layers of complexity than we previously thought:

> *"I learned that some skills that I thought were innate–like the bullet-fast reactions of Major League hitters–are learned, and others that I thought were entirely voluntary acts of will, like the compulsive drive to train, have important genetic components. I learned that the best genetic and physiological research in sports often contradicted my intuition about elite sports performance."[21]*

So Epstein discovered that even traits like willpower are in some ways affected by your genetics. Like horses in horseracing and sprinters in sprinting, some have the breeding to fit certain sport's particular demands. In fact, it is interesting to witness bespoke training programs now being devised worldwide, based on an individual`s specific DNA profile. For instance, Ian Craig – a British exercise physiologist – has developed DNAFit tests which enable athletes to gain some understanding of their genetic makeup, thus appreciating which type of sport they are more likely to accrue success.[22]

The DNAFit tests base their results on a certain number of genes (approximately 20-25), and demonstrate that specific genes, and variations of them, are associated with different responses to training. For example, the ACTN3 gene is associated with power; the PPARA gene is linked to the regulation of fat; and a predisposition of the ACE II gene means carriers have greater VO_2 max potential (the maximum rate at which oxygen can be utilized by the body during exercise). And there are many more performance genes that influence what sports athletes are likely to be good at, and how they should be structuring their training. Many coaches now even

suggest that in the quest to determine athletic potential in all sports, DNA profiling should become something that is universally adopted.

The beauty of game sports however is that there are so many facades to the sport that gains can be made in many areas, not only the technical, psychological and tactical areas. Understanding genetics is where the shrewd coach and parent may thrive by encouraging pathways based on natural individual talents.

Before you fly: Reflections

This was quite a lot of information to begin with. Maybe it will take a little time to settle in, or maybe you knew most of it already. If you found it useful, then write anything that you feel will make a difference to you below:

The Doctor and the Academic!

Research, classic observations, repeated mistakes and ideas

In this chapter you are presented with two discussions. Bryan Jones and Dr. Ian Horsley are vastly experienced professionals in the area of sport. With strong academic backgrounds and vast ranges of applied experiences working with young performers and their families, both share excellent blends of knowledge and wisdom.

Discussion 1 - The Academic: Bryan Jones

Me: What does sports coaching research suggest is important about effective sports parenting?

Bryan: *In terms of brand new research, there isn't much different from the ideas coming out since the 1990's. We knew then as we do now that the motivational climate a parent is part of setting up is of most importance, as children get to the competitive levels of sport. For children to continue to thrive and participate in sport, research has shown that they need to maintain enjoyment of their sport; and their self-esteem within that sporting context needs to remain strong. Clearly, parents impact both of these areas by how they involve themselves with their children and their sport. Those parents who appropriately involve themselves do best.*

Me: What is the most appropriate or best way then?

Bryan: *Well, this is not a clear cut answer; and this is where we have improved our thinking. A lot depends on the children and how they perceive their parents' involvement. Much depends on the culture of the family and much can depend on the sport itself. This is called a multidimensional approach, and although it can be complicated it is perhaps the most realistic way of thinking about leadership and relationships.*

Here is an example:

The researcher J. C. Hellstedt classified parental involvement in sport as being *under-involved, moderate,* or *over-involved.*[23]

Involvement Level	Characterized by
Under-involved	Low levels of interest, investment of minimal time, low financial help for equipment, not interested in finding funds to support, don't engage with coaches concerning their child's development.
Moderate involvement	Firm but fair with their children. Flexible outlook with motivational approaches and using incentives for goal setting with their child, mainly inspiring. Allows decision making concerning their child's sport to be made by the child themselves. Seeks advice and feedback from the coach about their child's development, and understands that they are not the coach but a parent. Emotional and financial support when required but not over the top or limitless.
Over-involved	Overemphasize victory, struggle with defeat as if it is personal. Much of their own self esteem dependent on sporting success of child. Tend to set unrealistic goals and pursue them as if it is their personal redemption for their own lost dreams. Visualize financial rewards and educational offers such as scholarships. Monitoring of most practice sessions and step across into role of coach.

These are three useful and simple ways of thinking about parental involvement. Everyone can recognize these parents and it is easy to classify them in their usefulness. We think moderate involvement is best and the other two are poor.

Me: Yes, as if the goal is to always be moderately involved because that is the best way to be.

Bryan: *Exactly. If only it was that simple. Research by Sabine Wuerth, and colleagues, discovered that what mattered most significantly was how each child internalized their parent's involvement.[24]* **Some children found one type of parent involvement really supportive and wanted it, yet other children found the same involvement stressful and upsetting.**

Me: I have noticed this for years. All different types of involvement have yielded all sorts of results with children. Siblings react completely differently to the same type of involvement and it is a common frustration of parents I talk to.

Bryan: *Yes, so over involvement to one person is one thing but appreciated by another. It is all about how it is perceived by the child and the bottom line is how they react. If they react positively to your involvement then we can call that healthy. If the involvement is damaging and creating stress then clearly it is unhealthy and needs changing.*

Example:

> Recently, I was in Egypt and watched a coaching session with a young girl about 8 years old. Her parents were both there watching and shouting at her to try harder. Each time she looked out she seemed to try harder than before, and at times broke out in laughter. When she came off court, both parents were warm with her and extremely supportive. She seemed very happy with the world.

Me: Do children need hardening up though to deal with what others are like? That all seems to be on the child's terms?

Bryan: *Well this is the balance that needs to be struck. Multidimensional Leadership Theory[25] proposes that although people have preferred leadership styles, certain situations demand a certain type of leadership.*

In basic terms, leaders are expected to vary their leadership style according to two sets of equally potent and at times conflicting forces:

1. **Situational demands** - *What does the situation require here? Example: a child needs to be told strongly what to do because of the safety risk.*

2. **Members preferences** - *How do the players like to be led? What do they prefer a leader to be? Example: Players like to be in charge making their own choices, but they enjoy support and direction when they ask for it.*

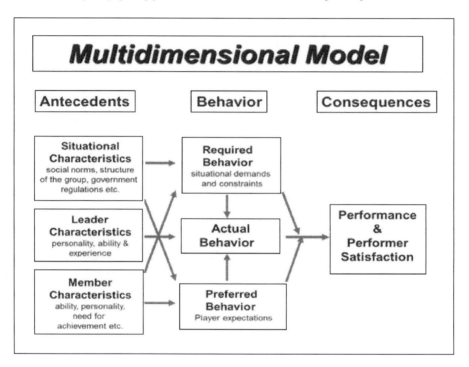

Dr. Packianathan Chelladurai's Multidimensional Model of Leadership[26]

Dr. Chelladurai – a renowned scholar in management science and organizational behavior in the context of sport – proposed that there are five types of leadership behavior:

1. **Training and instruction:** *Behavior is aimed at improving performance.*

2. **Democratic:** *Allows decisions to be made collectively.*

3. **Autocratic:** *Gives the leader personal authority.*

4. **Social support:** *Shows concern for the wellbeing of others.*

5. **Rewarding:** *Provides team members with positive reinforcement.*

Parents who can show the adaptability and skill to match their leadership style with what the situation requires and what their child prefers are likely to have a healthy impact on them both in the short-term and the long-term. This is difficult to always achieve, but is a more realistic way of thinking about leadership and is useful for sports parents and coaches.

Me: That makes a lot of sense and is why relationships are an ART not a science. *Speaking of the long-term, are there any long-term psychological skills that parents can use to directly help encourage the children through sport and school?*

Bryan: *Absolutely yes. Some recent work from the University of Central Lancashire has addressed this issue directly. Áine MacNamara & Professor Dave Collins have proposed certain Psychological Characteristics of Developing Excellence (PCDE's).[27]*

Psychological Characteristics of Developing Excellence (PCDE's) established in the literature are:

- *Competitiveness*
- *Commitment*
- *Vision of what it takes to succeed*
- *Imagery*
- *Importance of working on weaknesses*
- *Coping under pressure*
- *Game awareness*
- *Self-belief*
- *Effective and controllable imagery*
- *Focus and distraction control*
- *Realistic performance evaluation and attribution*
- *Role and clarity commitment*
- *Planning and organization*
- *Goal-setting and self-reinforcement*
- *Quality practice*
- *Resilience*
- *Creating and using support networks.*

These have been identified as the most important characteristics that will help youngsters move towards excellence in sport. Some performers start off with different strengths and weaknesses in each area, and it is through coaching, parenting, and socialization that we can help young people to grow and develop such characteristics to optimal levels.

Me: This reminds me of much of the *Emotional Intelligence* work made popular by psychologist Daniel Goleman[28] and the *Growth Mindset* ideas of Professor Carol Dweck.[29] Both emphasize the need to develop emotions and character in people as a main priority.

Bryan: *Yes, whereas PCDE's are sport specific. All these things emphasize the importance of considering the long-term psychological and emotional development of people. A common problem in sport is that we only value what we can see, in the physical skills; but if we only consider the development of only what we can see, we aren't molding young people for the tougher challenges ahead, nor are we appreciating all the opportunities to build character and praise children for showing it.*

Me: Can you give an example of one?

Bryan: *A good one is **resilience**. If young persons are to be encouraged to develop resilience, there must be elements of failure present in their lives. They must learn how to cope and to reinterpret what failure means to them. We as coaches and parents can allow them the space to feel the failure for a while, and then let them deal with how they choose to react. We can encourage the effort to go again, to 'get back on the horse', but we must be careful about how many times we physically put them back on the horse. Ideally, **they** have to choose to do it.*

*We need to limit the excuses and sympathy but converse with them if they want to discuss the failure they feel. This way they will learn how to deal with setbacks themselves, and as time goes on this will become part of their mental skillset. As parents, if you notice this going on, you can give much positive reinforcement and let them know you value this mental skill as much as any other skill they perform. If they come back in tough situations, keep training well when it's tough, maintain optimism during poor form, or make positive appraisals of where they need to improve, **notice these things. They are developing resilience for themselves.***

Me: So is this where promoting doing well at school is important too? Adam Henley (professional soccer player for Blackburn Rovers Football Club) told me this was very important to him in his character development and ability to play soccer in the English Premier League. Here is what he said:

Adam Henley:

My mother has always been supportive and helped me and my brother become independent. She emphasized that schoolwork was a priority, and homework had to be done. This was huge in my development because when you're young you don't understand how important it is to overcome problems and learn to stick with things you may not naturally like. You may think 'math is just math', but it isn't just math. It is problem solving and improving the way you think, as other subjects do. You've got to be able to figure things out, and you've got to become self-aware of what makes you tick, so that you can deal with all the problems that come your way when you're trying to make it. So schoolwork can develop maturity and resilience, and this can potentially help you become a successful player. You've got to be resilient in life and school can help with that a lot. So I'm really glad my mother was strict with us about school.

It's not just the work you do, it's the attitude schoolwork breeds. It taught me how to focus and 'get my head down' on things I didn't necessarily want to do. Just recently I've had to buckle down and improve lots of things in my game. It has taken lots of discipline to do it but I have a confidence I can do it because I learned how to at school. If I had been let off at school by everyone and it was like: "Oh Adam is probably going to get a professional contract", I wouldn't have learned that self-awareness and discipline.

Bryan: *Well simply, parents who promoted school achievement in academic and sporting terms as being more important, or at least of equal importance, tended to help their children in all areas of their future. School is simply another form of challenge that in many ways needs to be dealt with positively. The challenges of academia, sport, and life for that matter are all the same. Lots of one's self-image is set when one is younger, and that relates to one's sense of intelligence, resilience, problem solving capability, discipline, and confidence in learning. So schoolwork can be vitally important to some in setting in stone positive self-expectations for the rest of one's life. Only in the investment years may there be a little more slack as the child's energy really pushes for elite sport.*

Me: How can coaches/parents push excellence while not being controlling?

Bryan: *Hellstedt, who was one of the first researchers to look into parental influences on sports competition, basically said that a **firm parental direction with enough flexibility to let the youngster have significant involvement in their decision making** was the best way to go.[30] In any performance domain one has to be good at making decisions and seeing them through. It builds self-confidence in that area even if it sometimes happens to be the wrong decision. Maybe one of the reasons some individuals struggle to become* *winners is because coaches and parents don't let them make real choices about how they want to play the sport; often preventing them the opportunity to solve tactical problems, decide how they train, and even how much level of commitment is needed to achieve success. If they hit some struggles through their choices, so be it. With a good supportive environment around them, they will learn how to ask for help when needed and not be faced with things the other way around when they're bombarded with everybody else's solutions. Don't deprive them of the struggle, as I like to say.*

Me: That must be difficult for parents though. It is natural to want to take away problems for them if you can?

Bryan: *It is hard, yes. I have it with my own daughter who is playing a lot of sport now. My daughter has to ask for what she wants, if she isn't happy with certain elements. She is busy with lots of projects and things and can't commit to everything all the time, so again I ask her how she wants to play it? She knows she can't do it all, so choices need to be made. I think that the essence of a winning mindset is one who can make decisions under pressure and get used to feeling the responsibility and consequences of such decisions.*

Me: How can parents and coaches work together to support the child better through all the stages on the sports journey?

Bryan: *Parents invest a lot of time and effort in supporting their children, and naturally they are concerned that there is some benefit to that. I go through that as a parent myself. A good coach wants to know that the parents also are happy. Problems come when there is a lack of coherence between parents, players, and coaches. A simple way of saying it is that 'they are not singing from the same hymn sheet.'*

*Anne Pankhurst's (Coach Education Consultant) research in this area suggests that all stakeholders in a child's development need to have similar perceptions (and therefore similar behaviors and reinforcement/support systems) of all the key elements of development.[31] If this doesn't happen, blame starts to emerge. You then get the **blamer, victim, and rescuer** dynamic going on.*

Me: Yes. Where there is a drama, you tend to get a person feeling like a victim of someone who has been the persecutor or blamer. This opens up the chance for a rescuer figure to come in and quite often blame the blamer! Generally, this circle of drama continues in a negative spiral. An example is when a parent blames a child for not winning, and the child feels like a victim and is rescued by the coach, who in turn blames the parent for inappropriate evaluations and behavior.

Bryan: *There are three main types of congruence that can really help reduce the occurrence of these dramas you talk about:*

*1. **Philosophical congruence** - this is sharing of the main values and beliefs and forming some common ground. For example, if we all value effort and enjoyment above results then we have a much better chance of not blaming each other when form goes poor but effort remains high. If enjoyment disappears then again we can as a team address it immediately. If we all believe that a certain way of playing the sport is the way to go, then again we have a better chance to stay loyal to that approach despite the ups and downs.*

*2. **Phenomenological congruence** - this is related to HOW the coaching is put together such as content of sessions and which things are being worked on. If all three parties agree and understand the rationale behind the type of coaching (e.g. how it is being planned and how much quantity is requested) then again there is much less chance of the victim and blamer scenario.*

*3. **Epistemological congruence** - this is a shared understanding of the process of learning and how it is achieved over periods of time. For example, if you believe in observational learning (watching and copying people) then there will be an understanding that training with role models and watching demonstrations and expert players is a useful process. If you believe in classical conditioning more, you will be looking to include more punishment and reward systems with lots of repetition. So the way you view the learning process is an area that really needs to be shared, so everyone is happy with the journey and trust in the process being applied.*

So the trick is to find a coach that can talk to you about these three areas and you can all find some common understanding of the methods being used and the vision you share. This should give you a better chance of you all being on the same page as Anne Pankhurst suggests, thus reducing that background tension and increasing positive energy.

Stability zones

Me: You talk a lot about stability zones. Can you elaborate?

Bryan: *As youngsters, when it comes to our parents we like to make them happy. It's like "if you're happy with me then I am happy." This goes on throughout our lives. So when kids go out and perform at a sport, they want to look at their parents and feel that they are enjoying watching them perform. If this is generally the case, the parent becomes a stabilizing influence. Sport becomes a place of effort, enjoyment, and pride; A stability zone. If the parents display disappointment or look unhappy, they become destabilizing, and the child is affected negatively. Sometimes the child perceives the parents to be disappointed even when they're not, but it's too late. They feel pressure to increase their performance or they won't have happy parents.*

Now occasionally this can work as a positive, it gives the child a 'kick up the backside' and effort can increase, leading to a better level of performance or even a victory for the child. However, if this is used as a method all the time it will eventually create negative associations with sport and will lead to a long term negative spiral. The child believes: **"Your happiness and therefore my happiness depends upon me performing well at sport according to your standards."**

BE CAREFUL

This premise of being dependent on the child's performance influencing the parent's feelings of gratification or dejection has also been termed the *'reverse-dependency trap'* by sport psychology researcher Frank Smoll,[32] and can be extremely disruptive for a child's experiences in the sport if it starts to spiral out of control.

Key influencers and Social Learning Theory

Me*: Do you then need to put a plan in place to help build these stability zones?

Bryan: *Yes, you do need a strategy. This is a hard thing to get right because instinctively parents want their kids to win in competition. This goes back to the Instinct Theory of Motivation[33] which has elements of truth, though quite partial. So observing one's child compete is instinctively a difficult thing to stay calm about, but we know from Social Learning Theory[34] that it is important to do just that. According to Social Learning Theory it is important that multiple reinforcements from significant others occurs if one is to create change. So,* *both parents, teachers at school, grandparents, siblings, coaches, and role models are vital in creating a consistent and reinforced social message. All these key influencers including their friends and parents of those friends, are significant in socializing a child. Clearly some have more weight of influence than others and the trick is to get the central message across on a consistent basis. Problems occur where mixed messages are being received by the child. For example: two parents arguing on the approach or a coach and a parent having different behaviors and views around performance.*

It would be wise to set up informal and sometimes formal meetings with each other so that the shared messages can be set and made consistent. This way you get a stable climate that the youngsters have the very best chance of developing themselves within.

Me: So what is recommended to parents then in order to create more stability?

Bryan: *Well the main thing is to assess your own values as a parent. If you do not value such things as support, love, independence, and enjoyment of sport, it is highly unlikely parents will display behaviors and attitudes that back that up.*

If they have such values and are keen to behave in a way that supports those values, they can achieve it. Some simple ideas are worth trying such as:

*1. **Let them play on their own for a while**. Drop your child off, wish good luck, and tell them to enjoy it and you can't wait to hear about it later. Solitude has proven to be a powerful aid in reflection and growth of independence. This is not abandonment, it is space for you and for them.*

*2. **Ask how the game went and if they enjoyed themselves**. If they want to talk about it let them, if not then talk about something else or just let it go.*

*3. **Don't make the car journey an analysis room!** If they do talk about it, listen fully. Do not offer too many solutions or be too analytical. Be interested by asking them to expand or offer concise advice IF THEY DIRECTLY ASK FOR IT. Have a set time and then get used to switching subjects or having fun another way in the car. NEVER SULK!*

4. *If you do watch, keep reminding yourself why you love them as your children*. See the person not the performer as much as you can. If you genuinely feel that love and respect for them, it will show in your body language naturally. Clap, encourage, and let them know you are happy.

5. *Buddy up with another parent you trust, so you can keep an eye out for each other*. Sometimes you can't hear your own negativity but you can hear another parent doing it. This will help teach you what you can be like and how damaging it comes across. You can also remind each other to have a quick re-check if one of you starts becoming over-zealous.

6. *Uphold agreed boundaries*. If your child goes too far and breaks agreed rules, displays unsporting behavior, or demonstrates a clear lack of effort then it is appropriate to confront them about that and press home the agreed consequences. It is not about being soft but being fair and enforcing agreed expectations related to behavior and effort.

7. *Not too high, not too low!* Avoid getting too emotionally high or too emotionally low after results. Simply, it must not affect you too much. The children need to know that you are relatively stable emotionally, no matter what the outcome.

Me: Yes, after a perceived big win I see lots of junior performers becoming the family headline news for a few weeks, especially with Twitter and Facebook now. The kids provide status to the parents socially it seems.

Bryan: *Yes, it goes beyond the right amount of pride. It is unstable. It changes the emphasis subtly and again parents must acknowledge success but in the right way. It's also important to celebrate small achievements such as improved effort, dedicated training, and continued enthusiasm. You must show you value these things just as much as victory moments if you want to create stability.*

Me: Many believe that the child won't have the motivation to win if they never get criticized or have things too stable. What do you say to this?

Bryan: *No research has proven this, although dealing with adversity does seem a common trait in many of those who make the grade professionally. Nothing has been proved to suggest that children have progressed because of* *unstable emotional environments, but we have seen studies show direct links to long-term negative psychological issues such as depression, self-abuse, and low self-esteem. Children who have faced emotional blackmail from parents have succeeded in spite of their parents, as opposed to positive consequences of this approach. Such children were good anyway and may have gone on to be even happier in life had the parent been less controlling. Andre Agassi is an example who springs to mind.*

Me: Lastly, can you give some simple ideas that you feel could help sports parents improve their effectiveness?

Bryan:

*1. **Know yourself better** - Parents can be an amazing resource for their children if they are self-aware enough to know when to dip in and help and when to back off. I don't buy into the standard line that many National Governing Bodies say parents should just shut up and stay away. Parents can be educated with the help of the coach and brought in to help where they can.*

*2. **Engage in dialogue with coaches** - Good coaches will be able to explain their philosophies and enjoy helping one to deal with the journey better. Thank coaches for their efforts because coaches can be fragile themselves deep down and recognition of their efforts and skills goes a long way. Of course, children should be encouraged to do the same when they feel they have been well coached.*

*3. **Use your relevant expertise** - If you have something to offer in the way of relevant expertise then find a way to be involved. Many parents have been brilliant at passing on knowledge and know how to inspire their children because of their past experiences as a performer or professional person. The trick is to have the self-awareness to realize when your input is detrimental. That is hard because one day your input is well received and the next day it is seen as negative interference! Sometimes you are dammed if you do and dammed if you don't, but never give up your support and understanding.*

*4. **Improve yourself first** - Working on yourself and adding bits of knowledge and emotional intelligence is learning that never ends. You can help them much more by consistently exhibiting the behaviors you want to see in them. Talk is cheap, and children learn far more from who you are and what you do* than what you preach! So to read books, talk to experts, buddy up with other parents, or take courses in self-development shows that you are prepared to change and grow too, which is a positive example you are setting.

Discussion 2 - The Physiotherapist - Dr. Ian Horsley

Me: Let's start with the positive. What have some of the most effective parents been like?

Ian: *They are calm and only really speak when invited to. They trust their kids to talk for themselves with the other adult in the room. I ask a question like "where are you feeling it hurt?", and they allow a conversation to emerge between us. They in contrast just listen quietly, or if their child asks them what they think, give a little information, but encourage their child to express themselves more clearly.*

They ask their children, "Do you want to?" They assume that their kids have to make their own decisions and basically give them a choice. That is important because it puts the responsibility back on the youngsters to live by their choices. They have to do the rehabilitation or whatever I suggest, so it makes sense that they are the ones who make the decision to listen to me or not! The best parents are like good friends rather than like parents. They come in like equals, without much stress or worry.

They are good at drawing out positives from tough situations. They have sympathy for their child but don't get dramatic themselves. They may say, "Oh well, that's not the best news, but at least you can have a good rest now and see your friends for a while", or "We can use some of the money we will save on going on a good holiday in summer."

They seem to have a life away from their child's sport. They appear to be happy people who care about their children and their sport, but it doesn't consume them. They have their own hobbies and interests too with friends outside of the social clique of the sport.

Me: You have treated many international level performers. Are there any common traits you have seen in these athletes that you think contributes to their success?

Ian: *If they can talk freely for themselves, then generally they are happy, and they exude confidence. If they struggle to talk without parents being there, they seem unhappy, which is a problem. They drive themselves on and thrive off the challenges. They know dealing with injury and rehabilitation is just part of the profession, and they get on with it.*

They actually listen to their support experts. So they show a trust in your opinion and go down the route you have suggested after a good discussion. I believe to be able to trust our advice shows strength of character. The really elite ones go and get the work done! They are meticulous in their work, and the motivation for it comes from within and knowing it will make them better in the long-term.

Me: On the negative side now, what are some of the repeated mistakes you have witnessed parents make over the years?

Ian: *Well it's the opposite of lots of the things I have just talked about. It is not good for parents to live vicariously through their children. There comes a point where the parent is so invested in their children's sport that the pressure to pay them back becomes huge. Winning becomes the only way of paying them back for all their time and money. They just want to make their parents happy deep down, but not everyone can win. So in a way they are caught in a situation they want to get out of but can't do so. They feel they owe their parents so much that they cannot just stop. So they keep going out of guilt but don't actually know what they feel. Then you hear comments like, "You're so ungrateful for all our support!" One of the worst thing parents do is talk out loud about all the hours they have driven and all the training sessions they have paid for as if it were a badge of honor. That piles on the pressure.*

Me: Yes, as if they are saying, 'I have done my part now you go and do yours and win'.

Ian: *That's it. It's like they need payback for their sacrifices.*

Me: Do you see that having direct consequences on their health and fitness?

Ian: *I have seen many fake injuries where I know the player is looking for a way out because of the pressure. I am not always sure this is a conscious thing but when we feel pressure and that turns into stress it is amazing how many strange injuries surface.*

Me: Wow that is interesting.

Ian: *It happens, and it is a way out of the pressure. It becomes the convenient backstory that everyone can deal with, and over time it reduces expectations which helps the performer. Sometimes they come back well, but often it leads to masking the problem and not getting to the root of it.*

It can be very difficult as a physiotherapist because you know what the problem might really be but you can't come out and say it because you have no direct proof. It is not a physiotherapist's job to get involved with family dynamics: It is up to the parent to be wise and sense what is happening. This is why I suggest that taking a step back to see the bigger picture is really important.

Me: So then sometimes you almost have to be a counselor with young players and their parents?

Ian: *Yes, I would say that is true. You get embarrassing situations with the child and parent arguing in front of you. You get the feeling that the child is trying to let you know how much pressure their parents put on them and at the same time tell them. This is sensitive, especially in teenage years when they start to want their own identity. Some parents need to look out for this and let the kid have room. I know that when my own two girls hit their teenage years, they believe they are independent and more mature than they are. You have to try and encourage that, and within agreed limits allow them to make their own decisions and live with the consequences. It isn't easy though to let go when you can foresee your children running into a few problems.*

Me: So how would you suggest family members can help the psychological aspects of injury and recovery?

Ian: *To a youngster or indeed any performer, their next performance is always the most important one. Those parents who can help their children understand the bigger picture and help them see beyond the next competition into their futures are most helpful. They are communicating that they* **care more for them as persons and their health much more than they care about some sports results.**

Young athletes have time on their side and parents can help by reminding youngsters of this instead of adding to the pressure by demanding quick remedies. There is a lot of pressure put on young kids to play for this team or that team. Funding and selection is often used as a pressure by other parties, so a parent who can resist this pressure and help their children realize the philosophy of long-term health is going to help.

Regeneration through rest and recovery time is vital. Rest isn't just physical rest and more sleep; it is rebalancing one's whole life. *The less stress one has cognitively, the better one's regeneration. Therefore it is crucial* *that one's family has a calming effect and not a stressful one. Sometimes, they must encourage total escape from their children's sport and allow them to do things youngsters do even if it seems contradictory to resting. If they want to go off playing another sport or they want to just go out messing about with their friends, then accept it. Put all the equipment away, don't talk about it, do other things.*

*The parents need to be able to break free of it all too, not one talking about the sport whenever they get the chance. The parent has to have a life too that doesn't revolve around one's child's sport. Only when children want to play again **because they are hungry** should they go back.*

Me: Is there an age that is best for the young performers to be left to manage their injuries and rehabilitation requirements a little more independently?

Ian: *It could be different for everyone because everyone has different relationships with their parents, and all mature at different ages. Generally speaking, it just becomes a slow letting go as the years pass, still supporting lots, but allowing the children to take the wheel more often. In fact, the time when they start driving a car is a natural transition because they can come on their own then. That is a time to really allow that independence to grow. It is important to relax the reins though because youngsters need to start taking responsibility for listening to and taking charge of their own injuries more. They are the only one who can do the work because it is their body, not their mother's or their father's.*

Me: Ideally, what do you think parents can do to support the young performers you treat in the best way?

Ian: *Put a focus on performance not winning. If you get wrapped up in the winning and losing too early it's a trap you can't get out of because your ego goes up too much and it becomes like a drug. So don't think about winning and losing in the first place, think about effort to win and enjoyment of competition as the priority.*

Me: Have you got any practical advice for sports parents from the physiotherapy perspective?

Ian: *Maturity and expectations. Due to the fact that they all mature at different ages, it is hard to know how things will turn out as they grow. Sometimes one can be good at a sport when one is 10 years old, but by the time one is 16 one's body has changed and one is better suited to another sport or* *position in the team. Yet people persist with what they were good at when 10 years old.*

*An **example** is that if one is short and heavy at 10 years old, one may play prop position in rugby and be good at it, yet at 16 when one is tall and slim one may be better in another position. If one stays in the skills set of a prop all the way through one's teens because that's all one thought one was good at then, it is very difficult to change at 16 even if one wants to. One has missed years of decision making skills and hand skills that other positions require. We should not box children in at young ages, but keep them playing all sports and trying different positions because one never knows how they will turn out after maturing.*

BE CAREFUL

This is something frequently observed in youth team sports in the U.S. For instance: In soccer many coaches 'pigeon-hole' youngsters into set positions week after week during the formative stages of their development – and usually this is done because short-term results take precedence over the long-term welfare of the athletes. But as Dr. Horsley recommends, it is imperative that youngsters are exposed to different positions so they enhance their capabilities in a variety of areas – especially those involved in team sports such as soccer, basketball or football etc.

It is important to understand the problems that growth spurts can cause. And it is important to educate the youngster about this and how limb length changes affect their balance and coordination skills which then knocks off their rhythm and so on. These spurts can be on and off for many years, and they can cause injuries also; so parents and coaches just need to relax about this and again see the bigger picture. If they need to take a step back and rest a while or not play as much, they should do.

Me: Yes, this issue is often overlooked in youth sport generally, and may explain why many young athletes struggle with their coordination skills from time to time. It is also interesting to observe the thoughts of Manchester United's Head of Athletic Development Tony Strudwick on this topic too, as he concurs with your view:

"When they have that peak growth spurt, they're going to lose coordination; so you need to monitor those things over the years. Don't always look at performance now: You've got to try and look at the whole athlete from physical, technical, tactical and psychological perspectives."[35]

Ian: *Act on the advice you've paid for.* *Take into account the rational reaction one would have if the advice given was being given to another child. This helps to have a more supportive reaction to the recommendations being given by the expert one has paid to see.* **Would you throw $50 out of the window in the parking lot? That's what many parents might as well do when I give them advice. Their heads nod in approval, but their eyes say, "No chance!"** *I recommend my professional view which usually involves rest and regeneration exercises, but parents are often looking for a 'quick fix' from me. I am there thinking of their son's or daughter's long-term health, and they are thinking about some ranking points or school competition they MUST play in!*

Injuries happen, superstars are rare. *The very best performers are extremely rare. Not everyone can become a superstar by design. Let go of the illusion that you can create champions by forced design and throwing money at it.* **There is a lot of natural genetics at play with some people and a lot of luck that they find the sport which works for them.** *Of course hard work pays off, and you can do lots of things to reduce chances of injury, but sometimes there aren't any solutions or reasons why injuries happen or surface again. There are elements of chance and luck to this process too, so don't expect things to be always fair; sport and the body's reaction to it doesn't work like that unfortunately.*

Me: Excellent practical advice. Anything final you feel is important?

Ian: *Create happy and positive memories.* *Last thing is that you must keep the focus on freshness and compiling happy positive memories. Children should be growing a memory bank of happy and enjoyable moments every time they participate in a sport. Even the painful losses and tougher moments must be remembered as positive learning experiences not as misery or traumatic family events. When children become adults you want them to still love a sport so they keep up with it no matter what level they get to. If they have lots of happy memories of a sport, they will more likely keep it up.*

Summary

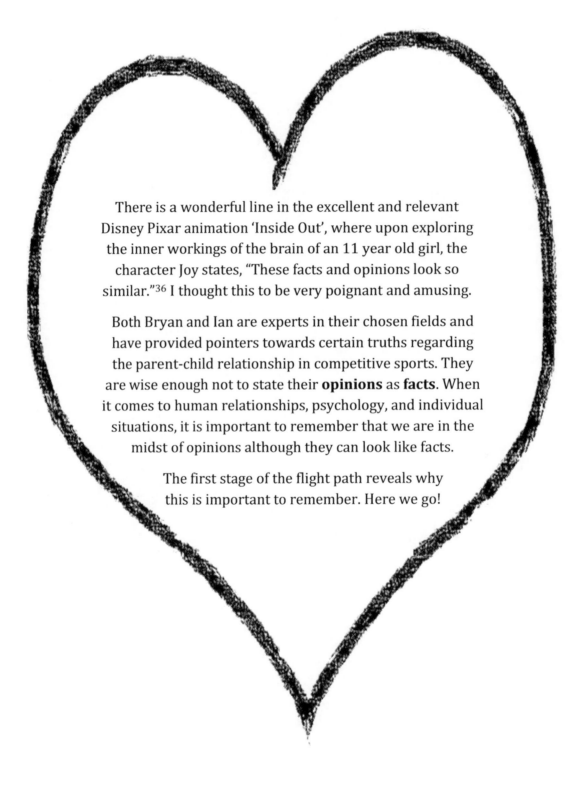

There is a wonderful line in the excellent and relevant Disney Pixar animation 'Inside Out', where upon exploring the inner workings of the brain of an 11 year old girl, the character Joy states, "These facts and opinions look so similar."[36] I thought this to be very poignant and amusing.

Both Bryan and Ian are experts in their chosen fields and have provided pointers towards certain truths regarding the parent-child relationship in competitive sports. They are wise enough not to state their **opinions** as **facts**. When it comes to human relationships, psychology, and individual situations, it is important to remember that we are in the midst of opinions although they can look like facts.

The first stage of the flight path reveals why this is important to remember. Here we go!

Notes & Reminders

Flight Path: Stage 1

'Self-Awareness'

Stage 1: Preparation for the Journey 'Self-Awareness'

This is the starting place of the flightpath, the time when it is important to check in with yourself and find out what skills and resources you need for your flight. Also, for those who have a fear of flying, it is time to admit it and find out why?

At this stage two simple questions need to be resolved before you can take off to new destinations with your children.

1. **Do you know what the areas are that you need to improve?**

2. **How prepared are you to change the way you think and behave?**

"The greatest discovery of our generation is that human beings can alter their lives by altering their attitudes of mind. As you think, so shall you be."[37]

William James, 19th Century Philosopher

I assume that by reading this book up to this point, some part of you has already realized there are things you can improve upon in the way you support your children through their competitive sports journey. If you do not believe you need to improve on anything, then read on till the end of this chapter and have a re-think.

Q. How many psychologists, coaches and trainers does it take to change a lightbulb?

A. Just one. But the lightbulb must want to change!

"Awareness is knowing what is happening around you; Self-awareness is knowing what you are experiencing. I am able to control only that of which I am aware. That of which I am unaware controls me."[38]

Sir John Whitmore

Stop exaggerating, Son.
I must've told you a million times!

Self-Awareness gives you power and at the same time takes away excuses linked to naivety and the assertion "I just didn't know!" **Awareness** of a problem is the beginning of the **solution.** In my own life it has been those 'aha' moments of self-awareness. Those times that I have realized what I've been doing without knowing it have really got my behavior changing. They are quite strange moments, a mixture of feeling stupid, embarrassed, and shocked. A noticeable dent in your self-image! One might think, "What have I been doing?" It's like the moment in the classic film 'It's a Wonderful Life'[39], where James Stewart is visited by his 'Guardian Angel' and shown how wrong he had perceived his life to be. Charles Dickens' wonderful character Ebenezer Scrooge[40] is cleverly made aware of how his day to day treatment of people will send him to an early grave! Both characters are made self-aware of the way they have been behaving, and it is only then that they go about a real change of attitude and behavior, from misery to joy in both cases.

BE CAREFUL

Unfortunately, some people only awaken though after it's too late. After a divorce maybe, or worse still, after a death of a loved one. This is one of the saddest things in life because usually it is too late to do the things and say the words you wish you had said. The trick is to wake up before it's too late and do something about it. Your children need you to improve NOW, while they are young sports performers. They don't need you in 10 years' time for this part of parenting.

A lack of self-awareness

The Drama Triangle: Blamer - Victim - Rescuer

As I indicated earlier in the book, what I witness most in the relationships between parent, coach, and player is an unfolding of a mini drama where there is generally someone blaming, someone playing the victim, and someone aiming to rescue the situation.

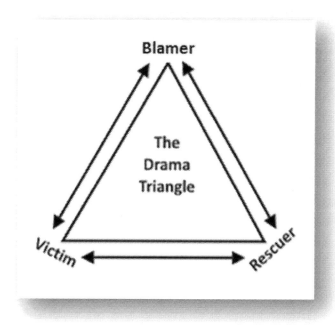

To illustrate this point, here is a letter I received from a parent *(a nice man with great intentions and who clearly wanted what was best for his son)* whom I had met on many occasions after he had brought his son to me for coaching. Read his letter and see if you can spot the blaming, rescuing, and victim parts?

Letter from parent:

Hi Danny,

I've just read your article, great work! Your own book, as with the others you have recommended me to read, is obviously going to be well worth reading.

I'm interested to know if there is anything you can send me to help with James' development. He's coming along nicely as a player, but has recently had a bit of a wakeup call - although he is ranked 3rd in our region, and 20th nationally, he failed to get picked for the Regional team which played the Junior Regional Championships last month.

Turns out being a lazy trainer at regionals cost him his place. It's not a great surprise. As a big fish in a small pond, he's not had to do that much to get where he is today. County champion, regional champion, impressive trophy cabinet etc. To be honest he suffers from a total lack of tough matches against other good kids at our club, and his training partner (mostly me) is simply not consistently good enough at feeding the ball to provide him with proper purposeful practice and technique improvement.

That said, he acknowledges the problem. He plays a boy in the semi-final of a tournament this coming weekend who beat him in a recent final, where he lost 11-9 in the fifth. Both of them scored the same number of points over the five games and the match lasted almost an hour. So very tough for both of them. James wasn't down about losing. He knew he'd tried his best to win, and a couple of ill-advised shot choices really cost him. But he takes risks, and I want him to, because one day he'll be good at the risky shots, and they'll be match winners.

I know his attitude is right. He views this weekend's re-match as an opportunity for early payback, and he's already playing U15 tournaments to get hard matches. By the way, he's just turned 12. He still goes to a top coach every week and he is pleased with his progress. I'm just looking for a bit more for him, and from him.

Any suggestions would be welcome. Hope to see you soon. Regards, Paul

Here is my response:

Paul, nice to hear from you.

I've had messages sent to me from parents practically all over the world similar to your email! Talented kids that don't seem to match with parents' 'keen as mustard' attitude.

I don't know what it is exactly, but I can't help but feel that the youngster is dominating the parents' emotions a bit much. They know deep, deep down that the parent will do anything to help them! The parent wants it more, and so many kids are being told they are lazy and don't do enough. As you say at the end, "I WANT more for HIM, from him!!!" It's got to be HIS WANT!

The sports child, although controlled and often shouted at, knows that the parent cannot bear the thought that the kid might not actually have the same level of drive as the adult. I've seen it over and over again. In the end parents can drive away the kids learning and internal motivation through blame, sarcasm, outbursts, and disappointed moods (apart from when he wins, and apart from when you're around people you don't want to see you behaving this way to him).

It's all based in what's called 'Self-Determination Theory'[41] and basically means motivation is better when it comes from your OWN unpressurized choices. How deflating is it when you get nagged at or told what to do? It can make you feel useless, demotivated, and controlled.

In your particular case my article is highly relevant. Re-read it and see if you can let James go a bit. Trust him more and get off his case. Emphasize school standards maybe, or perhaps try a new sport or hobby for a while. Support him when he asks nicely. Set strong ground rules that a son should have. Ask how he is feeling, and just love him. Let the coaches coach him; give him space. Let sport be HIS thing not yours. So many parents rob their kids of that feeling of independence; a sport they do away from parents, not a sport WE all do. It's all dressed up as BONDING, and of course it is; but it rarely promotes the self-motivation from within needed to GROW and DRIVE ON. It's all in the article really. IT won't be easy, but the simplest way I can say it is, "Back away a bit, and don't obsess too much about results and rankings". Think of the fun parts. I hope you're well, Danny

To this day, I never heard back from Paul. Can you detect the blamer – rescuer – victim pattern going on here? Re-read the two emails and see if you can pick out:

1. ***Who is being blamed?***

2. ***Who is being the rescuer?***

3. ***Who is acting the victim?***

Whoever you feel is the blamer, victim, or rescuer is not really the point I am trying to make; yet this is a very good exercise because as you try to work it out, you may begin to be reminded of interactions with your own children and their coaches.

At some stage we probably all feel like the victim, we all blame, and we all try and rescue too. The point here is that this particular parent **asked** for advice along the lines of the article I had written. I replied kindly offering some explanations and personal opinion. On reflection, it seemed less painful for this parent to look inside himself and change his approach, and much easier to blame his son or myself for bad advice! Did he not want to change himself? Maybe he wanted a quick fix mechanism to boost his lazy son's attitude?

Self-awareness can be embarrassing and a bit painful. It shines a light on yourself in a way that is uncomfortable, and it generally means you face a bit of 'home truth.'

How much are you prepared to change to get what you want? Are you prepared to take on some new levels of self-awareness so that you may alter your approach?

Responsibility

Realizing we need to change can be demotivating and can lead to defensiveness, denial, and closure to new ideas. It can feel uncomfortable, especially when somebody else has pointed it out to you in the form of advice. This is why increasing your self-awareness is so much better than receiving advice, because as renowned Performance Coach Sir John Whitmore succinctly points out in his best-selling book <u>Coaching for Performance</u>: *"If I give you my advice and it fails, you will blame me. I have traded my advice for your responsibility, and that is seldom a good deal."*[42]

It is the recovering alcoholic having to openly admit his dependency on alcohol and stop drinking, and the over enthusiastic coaches suddenly realizing they are more effective when they talk less and become quieter. It is the competitive sports parents seeing their own over-analytical behavior mirrored in another parent; **and it dawns on them they are doing exactly the same.**

In all these scenarios, the responsibility to change stays within the persons themselves. They have nobody to blame because no advice has been offered. This is vital because this is where change is far more likely to happen. If we link back to Ebenezer Scrooge, the skill of the visiting ghosts *(or life coach's as we could say)* was simply to **reveal** life as it was.[43] They gave no advice, no science research, or no quick fix gimmicks how to change. They simply reflected back a picture of his past life, present life, and probable future life if he stayed as he was. This ultimately instigated the positive change in Ebenezer Scrooge's behavior – specifically the way he treated people in his daily life.

"Pushy parent - Not me. I just want what's best for them!"

Nobody I have met labels themselves the 'pushy parent' that they easily tag others with. It amazes me how many parents have complained to me about **other** intense parents, yet don't realize they are creating the same effect with their own children but just in a different way.

I have come to believe that the main reason for this form of hypocrisy is because their own intrusive behavior is genuinely meant to be for the positive; for the *greater good, constructive criticism* that *you will thank me for one day*. Some of the time such involvement can be good, yet used most of the time the intrusion backfires. In the short-term there is little urgency to worry about looking for negative long-term effects of over-involvement and clever coercion. Even if it were noticed, who is going to help the parents understand what their over-involvement is creating in the psychology of their child? Most coaches rarely seek potential confrontations with parents since they get paid in finance and status. The parents see nothing wrong because they think they are helping create the superstar their child deserves to become and was born to be. The young performer certainly doesn't foresee problems because apart from being young (naïve), they are getting lots of attention, are often waited upon by adults, and positive recognition of achievement with the promise of more if they comply!

British swimmer & Commonwealth Games medallist Lauren Quigley:

One day I just said to my mother, "Look, I don't want to talk about my race when it's coming up; it just makes me worse. I know you're trying to help, but it's not. I am different from you: You used to like talking about it when you raced, but I don't." It was just telling her that what used to work for her didn't mean it worked for me. I think she was a bit shocked because she didn't say much. I explained this to Dad too, and I think he helped calm my mother down a bit.

Q. Why are so many of us blind to ourselves?

A. You do not know what you do not know!

How can you improve when you have no idea you need to improve, and never mind what you need to improve? Only when you do that will you have a **choice**! A choice to act and change, or a choice not to. In the case of parenting, I believe most of you will choose to act because when it comes to those we love we tend to do more, even more than we would for ourselves in most cases. When it feels like a personal choice and not an instruction, we tend to be more determined. I have seen really big transformations in some parents the moment they realize they had made their children cry, or become dejected with their sport through constant pressure. It took such a public meltdown to help the parent learn that their behavior resulted in their child becoming stressed. Until this point they really did not know how much they were upsetting their child, even though other people could clearly see it. Nobody had been able to tell them, so they did not know. "Why didn't you tell me?", they would say softly to their child later on. "I tried to, but you didn't get it. You don't know what it's like".

Can you blame a person then if they genuinely don't know what effect they are having? Well, how can you blame them? It would be like calling somebody stupid for not being able to see in a pitch-black room! They just can't see! However, we could blame them if they had been told the room would be pitch-black and that they should take a lit candle with them or even better turn on the light switch as they entered. Then we could blame them because they had a choice. They had an option to light up the room and make it much easier to find their way. This is the difference, and this is why the first stage of the winning flightpath is based upon the concept of **awareness.**

I hate this room!

1990: My first blast of self-awareness, responsibility and self-help

Aged 16, I lived by myself in a small apartment. With parents divorced a year earlier, circumstances prevailed that led me to be dealing with home life alone. I remember being excited by the opportunity when my mother suggested it to me quite casually one day. *"Yes, that will be brilliant. I'll be my own boss,"* I enthused.

It only took a few weeks to learn that being one's own boss is nothing to get excited about when you are young. I found the evenings and mornings particularly lonely. Going to sleep and waking up alone started as strange, and quickly escalated into sadness affecting my confidence. Contrary to what most people thought at the time when they heard I lived on my own, the challenge was more psychological than practical. Cooking, cleaning, and grocery shopping I could deal with, but I distinctly remember being lonely, bored, sometimes scared, and frequently demotivated. Often music and TV sports kept me going. Always one for a brave face, I told others it was the best thing that had happened to me; yet my education suffered as I missed classes and found it hard to have any drive. I did not know nor did I appreciate it at the time, but my solitude taught me my best lesson of all, and my most important education was in full flow.

It was a grey November Sunday when the electricity shut off in my apartment that started a chain of events which changed me. No TV, no music, no hot water, no phone, just me with the silence. I didn't know any of my neighbours, who all seemed strange to me. As the hours passed, I went for a little jog, came back but still no electricity. I sat there resigned, self-pity creeping in like an incoming tide. I got into bed, curled up under my single quilt, and started to cry. I felt frightened and lonely. I felt like a failure and I questioned what I had done to deserve this. Of course I found answers, answers that obliterated my self-esteem and sent me further into the comfort of my quilted cave.

I don't know how I stayed or how long, but oddly something in me sparked up;

"I am not lonely, I am just making myself lonely," I thought. "I'm deciding to feel this way."

"Yes, get up and do something. You are feeling sorry for yourself, you know you are. Move, do something useful. You're not ill, there's nothing wrong with you," rang a determined voice.

"Come on, get up. Let's do something useful. Let's get this place cleaned up before it goes dark. We can start with the kitchen and see how much we can get done before the electric comes back on. Race, challenge. Come on Danny, you're good at this when you want to be. Let's go, NOW!"

I think days alone brought into focus that I was having conversations with myself. I felt like I was making up my own company, as if there were two of me in my flat! My language flipped between "I, you and we"! I hoped I wasn't going a bit **'doolally'**, the local term for people who spoke to themselves out loud! I was genuinely pondering thoughts of my looming insanity over the next few days as myself and I teamed up! I need not have worried. As my apartment took shape, my mood and energy improved with it. When the electric surged back on late that night, it was nice but not overwhelming. I had generated my own energy that afternoon, a force that was free and always accessible to me if ever I wanted to tap into it. On reflection, I believe that particular Sunday in November and the days that followed allowed me to realize that I always had choices in my thinking. Therefore, if I could control my thoughts, I could control how I felt. I wanted to go and find out more. To be continued…

Building your self-awareness: Exercise One

Below are some of the common beliefs and complaints I have come across from sports parents. Do you experience any of these feelings and views?

- *I am only trying to help you; what is your problem?*

- *So what if I get involved a bit too much! They are my kids and I know them better than anyone else!*

- *They can't be trusted yet to work it out for themselves; they need ongoing support and information from me. It is a horrible world out there!*

- *I can really help them if only they would properly listen to me.*

- *I don't want them to repeat my mistakes and the missed opportunities I had.*

- *I believe they should repeat the strategies that worked for me through my life.*

- *I can't stand by and watch them fail (learn!) especially when I could have prevented it for them.*

- *It is my job to make sure they become successful.*

- *Why can't you be more like your brother/sister, they don't have this problem?*

- *It is my job to protect them from failure and misery in sport.*

- *They should be doing more of what 'x' is doing because they are winning more and of course winning more is good.*

- *We are in this together, we are a team and we can get there together. It's a good bonding opportunity for us!*

- *They are just like me when I was their age. I know they have the same desires and fears I had. So I can fix this.*

- *Let's get more experts involved, it can only help.*

- *I am sacrificing a lot for your sport, you should be better than what you are.*

- *The more they win, the happier they will be.*

- *The more they win, the more certain their future.*

- *The more they win, the more it proves I am a good parent.*

- *We are paying all this money to the coach and THEY aren't making my child better!*

Which ones made sense to you? Write down the ones that you felt the most empathy with, the ones you really believe are true.

Take a look at the ones you have written down and have a think whether these background beliefs are actually true. For example, if you chose **"The more they win, the happier they will be,"** is that actually true? Could it be possible that in the long-term they will become sad by never learning the skills of resilience, losing with dignity, and understanding that effort and performance is better to focus on than only winning?

Personally, I have seen many so called **big tournament wins** become like a heavy sack the child ends up carrying around with them as they get older and fail to regain the past glories of that past massive achievement when they were 13 years old. So challenge your unconscious **assumptions**. You may find that many of your fears and concerns will fall away, as you realize there are other ways of thinking about your child's development.

Observer position

When we do exercises like this, we get a chance to be honest with ourselves because we take a step back from daily pressure. From this position of observer, it is easier to notice that we may overdo things, in this case the control of your children's sporting adventures. Normally, everyone but you is an observer of your situation, and therefore it is more difficult for you to notice the bigger picture that others see clearly. On the flip side, the behaviors we see in others because we have a bit of distance are often so obvious to see. Their emotional outbursts or their disappointed and sulky withdrawals of attention are clear. Their instant expert analysis, their overeager need to fix things and take revenge on their child's sporting 'enemy', all look too intense. Their hurtful personal comments, sarcastic tone, their over the top celebrations, their over hyping of their own child, and the embarrassing abuse of officials, coaches, other parents, and the opposition; all fuel and maintain the cycle of pressure.

Such behavior is in direct contrast to that one would expect loving people to display. You would expect calmness, some light humor, and happiness if you truly loved someone. Here there is hope. I believe when we become better observers of ourselves and learn to take a step back we may improve our understanding of how we are actually behaving. We may start to understand the long-term consequences of our approaches to leading those we love, and change ourselves before it's too late.

Building self-awareness - Exercise two: The power of a good story

A story is powerful because it puts you into an observer's position. With less attachment comes less defensiveness and a more open, relaxed mind. Not feeling personally attacked, we can gain much awareness through reading an interesting tale. Try this one:

Tom's first day back to school

Tom woke early today, excited. It's the first day of the New Year, the new school year that is. Summer break was good, but Tom is ready for some structure again, not that he is aware of it or would admit it even if he knew. His brain is hungry for new information and eager teachers. The thought of a new timetable to follow is an energizing prospect and will be attacked with new pens, fresh books, and brand new black shoes. Tom thought to himself, ***"I wonder who'll be my teacher for Math class? I hope we get Mrs. Connelly for History, not Mr. Grimshaw, please not old Grimble!"***

His most pressing interest though was PE and the school soccer team. After a summer of playing soccer nearly each day and building confidence with new friends from the neighborhood, Tom was certain he would make the school team, which was everything to him.

Two minutes to finish his cereal, five minutes to do his hair, and 55 seconds to check his bag and make sure he has his phone in his pocket, Tom is ready! Impatient, he waits by the car, kicking the tires trying to get rid of some pent-up energy. "Come on we're going to be late," cried Tom.

"Wow, if only he could be this urgent every day," thought his mother.

Tom would walk if it were trusted to; some of his younger friends do but despite his many requests he is told it's not safe enough yet.

Ten minutes later they are approaching the gates. Tom senses it's all a bit busier than normal and he can't quite understand why he feels a bit claustrophobic. There are more adults about the yard, and the atmosphere is different. Before panicking, Tom assumes it's because he's been off for so long (six weeks feels like six months for him, aged 12 years and 129 days old), "This is fine mom, here, here mom, just over there then?"

It's embarrassing to Tom to be still cradled, but he loves his mother so he doesn't mention it, hoping instead that she will sense it. Unfortunately she doesn't, and to add to the misery she seems to be actually parking the car.

"Mom, its fine. I can get out here quickly."

Off goes the engine. "Oh no, this is grim," Tom pondered.

"Now I've got a surprise for you Tom," his mom beams.

"It's been decided by the school that if parents want to, they can choose to come along to the classes. We all think that if adults can come and help their children learn at school by watching and just helping out a bit, then the kids are bound to do better."

Tom sat stunned as if he'd suddenly been held up by robbers. In some ways he had. His mother, bursting with zest, talked on, "Now, your dad and I have decided that we will take it in turns to be with you at lessons, unless we are both available, and then we will both help. Don't worry about us giving our time up or quitting our own hobbies a bit; we are quite excited about it all, and we know you'll appreciate us. Besides, I might even learn something myself!"

Feeling hollow, Tom struggled to make a noise. The force of his mom's enthusiasm and the conviction in her that this was to be a natural thing to do rendered Tom's ability to express anything. "So... I mean....who...how much will....why...how long will you have to do that for?"

Still beaming, with Tom now noticing his mother more dressed up than normal for a Monday morning, Mrs. Crowther couldn't sense her son's distress. "Well, as long as you want, my darling."

Walking into the school playground was excruciating. Mrs. Crowther didn't attempt to hold her son's hand, but it didn't half feel like it for young Tom. Lacking in rhythm, his walk was slow. Other youngsters were the same. Strangely the play area appeared smaller and darker than he remembered it to be, a lot less noisy too. No screams or chasing about going on. Instead, this was replaced with tension in the air, false smiles and worried minds. It all condensed further as the school corridors filled up. Shuffling feet and suspicious eyes caught on, and spread like an early morning fog.

In class, it was clear some of the parents had opted out of the 'family together' scheme. Twelve children were seated alone on single desks with all their things out, ready to begin their learning adventure. To them it was equally strange to see so many adults in their space. Tom, miserable already, stared into space, feeling the initial effects of his robbery. Some relieved to be left alone, some confused, and some now wondering if their own parents were committed to them enough. This was weird. Some children had both Mother and Father helping the cause. In their wisdom, some sat at the back of the room, believing that sitting next to their child was too involved, too intrusive, and inwardly criticized those sitting within touching distance. "Look at Mr. Havealot, typically, right in there interfering too much," sneered Mr. and Mrs. Smith, who sat 4.6 yards away from their marvelous daughter.

As youngsters slumped slightly, adults sat at attention, alert and proud. Nobody was misbehaving; nobody on their phones when they needn't be; and certainly no abuse in the air. There was no flourished teasing, laughter, occasional threat, or flying missiles. No possibility of detention today, just no room for it; it was as if class had been transported to church, but without the pretty art to lighten the intensity.

Mr. Halshaw walked in the room on time, more upright though, stiffer, with less bounce. Tom was pleased to see him, eager to ask how he was and what had happened to his school. A teacher of eight years, 'Mr. H' loved his job, he had a knack for it, and it was easy to grasp that helping young people made his heart sing. Delivering math was his game, and he loved it. Always attending conferences, collecting books, and writing for exam boards, Mr. Halshaw was fascinated by his teaching topic. His repertoire for delivering mathematics at all different levels was particularly well-respected by his colleagues and more poignantly by his pupils. He wasn't just a math teacher, you see; he used his topic as a vehicle to enlighten his learners about life in general. A fantastic giving man, he earned respect and authority because of the magic way he went about making young people feel. He coached them to think by allowing them space; he praised effort far more than ability, and he let his learners struggle in order to facilitate their understanding. He rarely showed stress despite his huge output. His enthusiasm was so great for life and learning, it was virtually impossible to be bored in his classroom.

Naturally the children's grades were always close to their potential. This was strange to some because he never really strove for the best grades. He preferred to focus on enjoyment and making equations, numbers, and divisions sound like the most interesting and most important thing one could ever learn. He stressed how one's life would improve financially and socially through applying knowledge. He talked of a lifelong love affair with the subject and told his pupils how he hoped they would continue on to a university one day. Tom was now happier because he knew who his Math teacher was to be this year, until his attention was disrupted when his mother asked, "Have you got all your books out ready?"

At this juncture, it is important to reflect on your views.

- *Is this something you intuitively feel is a good idea?*

- *Would it be good to take the sports parenting model and apply it to school if you had the time to do so?*

- *What may be the long-term issues for Tom and his classmates?*

- *How do you think the teachers will be affected by the ongoing presence of parents in the learning environment?*

Back to the story:

"So who can tell me how much extra carpet they need to buy, now that the house has added the *six yards* extra extension and the front doorway area taken away?"

This was a tough one if you didn't get the simple formula.

"Come on guys, you can do this, use the formula we just played about with," continued the expert teacher.

As the young learners responded in their various forms, some hastily, some dazed and confused, some pretending to try, a tension built in the room, an unfamiliar one. There seemed to be more value in getting it right and more fear of getting it wrong. Due to this, there was hesitance to risk and perhaps fail. The ones that confidently knew the answer seemed more eager to shout it out. Less relaxation, less composure. Tom was in the middle; he was struggling to think straight and concentrate. Usually he relaxed and waited to learn from others who answered, and then he seemed to understand things. Utilizing peer learning was something he had become accustomed to, like many of the other children in the class. But today this option had been dampened discernibly. "Come on Tom, you've just got to break it down in parts and then use it all back up. You can easily do this," chirped his Mother.

"Ssshh, mom it's harder than it looks."

"Ok, I'm only trying to help. What do I know, eh?" (Laughter).

By this time there was a murmur of noise building with many parents unable to resist helping.

Mr. Halshaw asked, "Ok Sarah, what's the answer?"
Sarah, unaccompanied by a parent, a girl of moderate intelligence but lots of determination replied, "22 square yards?"

It was wrong.

Mr. Halshaw asked, "How did you come to that answer?"

"Well, if you take the extra six yards times the width which is 4 yards, you get 24. Minus... oh... no I've forgot the width of the doorway."

She realized her error.

"Good effort, but hopefully you can see now how easy it is to rush it sometimes and make such a simple miscalculation. Even Einstein had to check his equations over and over because he was prone to mistakes as a youngster," proclaimed Mr. Halshaw.

Sarah, undeterred learned the main lesson here was to get better at something. Mistakes are part of the process, and even a great like Albert Einstein was once a beginner.

This lesson slipped by many in the room as they obsessed over the correct response. Many didn't take on board or appreciate the value of Sarah's response. You didn't win by getting it wrong. Meanwhile Mrs. Crowther had drawn the equation out and shoehorned Tom into his instant enlightenment.

Mrs. Crowther spurted, "We believe we've got it here, don't we Tom?"

Tom not wanting to engage remained quiet.

Mr. Halshaw replied, "Ok, what've you got to Tom?"

As Tom gave the correct response, he continued to stutter his way through the process of how he had solved it. He just did enough to convince his teacher he had a grasp of it, but inside he knew he hadn't really.

"Well done, Tom, correct," Mr. Halshaw proclaimed to the group.

Mrs. Crowther suddenly glowed, "I knew he would be clever if he tried".

The rest of the parents knew what had gone on, Mr. Halshaw did too, and so did young Tom. Yet Mrs. Crowther was completely ignorant of yet another vital lesson that had unfolded before her.

At this point, let's take another moment to reflect:

- *How do you predict some of the other parents will now react as this culture of a parent/child schooling unfolds?*

- *What will happen to the atmosphere across the school as a result?*

This story emerged because I wanted to make a graphic illustration of the difference I have felt between a school's educational atmosphere and a sports-coaching setting. These days the divide hardly exists. I have been able to include parents in a much more effective way, but when I meet and coach with new families or observe youth competitions, the differences are huge. Whenever you are being observed or scrutinized doing your job, it is quite a strange thing. For coaches of little experience (under 5 -10 years), it can be very distracting and damaging to that person's natural flow. I have noticed that coaches don't relax in these conditions and are more likely to pander to possible criticisms coming from parental observers. The default reaction is the urge to over-coach and over-control in an attempt to convince the expectant onlookers that 'I know my stuff' and 'I really do care about improvement.' Coaches try to 'earn' their money more obviously. They play the 'role of coach' instead of simply being a coach. They become more instructor like and go with the premise of more information, more structure, and more involvement is better. This contradicts much of what coaching really is where less is often more, where questions and answers are skillfully given room to breathe, and where discussion is equal. Failure and experimentation are played with, attention is withdrawn and then magnified as you try to make them earn their own improvement.

It goes further too. The children themselves join in the act. They play up to the demands of the observers and often view success as in being good listeners and complying with the instructional demands. Everyone happy! Boxes ticked! Nowhere was this more evident than when I was a teacher observer, and observed as a teacher myself, during my personal experiences in education in the UK. The way educational experts have approached improvement in teaching standards is to watch a teacher deliver a lesson, and then give the teacher a grade, based on pre-set criteria. The view is that from that one lesson a teacher can be graded from outstanding to unacceptable. My view was that many teachers learned how to perform in such situations and those who did and who knew what the observers were looking for could generally 'switch on the charm' so to speak and impress the judges. Do we want 'performing seals' or do we want free minds that have learned by themselves what the consequences of their actions are? Authentic young people while being socialized still have the individuality, responsibility, and confidence to become their own persons and evolve into their natural style.

I'd like to leave you with these questions to think about:

- *Have you ever had ongoing observation and been criticized regularly at work by somebody you love? How does it feel?*

- *Have you been a better influence on your children by knowing less about their sport than knowing all the details?*

- *Why is your best friend somebody you are prepared to tell your fears? Has it anything to do with them not trying to 'fix you' and their ability to listen and to just be themselves?*

Self-awareness leads to greater flexibility

"The person with the greatest flexibility of thought and behavior tends to control the outcome of any interaction."[44]

British Psychiatrist William Ashby

This quote was inspired by William Ashby's 'Law of Requisite Variety'.[45] The point being that the more you can adapt your thinking and methods of relating with people, the more you will reach satisfactory outcomes.

Practical ideas to help your self-awareness:

1. As suggested earlier in the book, 'buddy up' with a trusted friend and help by watching and listening to each other at competitions. Make a few mental

notes and discuss it over a drink. You can also be there for each other at any point just to give each other a nudge if one of you are going off center! Over time, you will become more aware of your useful and not so useful tendencies.

2. Have a session with a personal coach who can help you reflect upon your impact as a sports parent? People who are neutral observers can ask important questions without it seeming personal.

3. Have a conversation with your child's coach and ask them the coach's opinion on how you are doing. This will help the trust between you and show you are not the problem parent coaches often presume.

4. Ask your children how you are doing as a supportive parent? This can be the best of all because your child will feel respected and heard, particularly if you take action on their feedback.

Summary

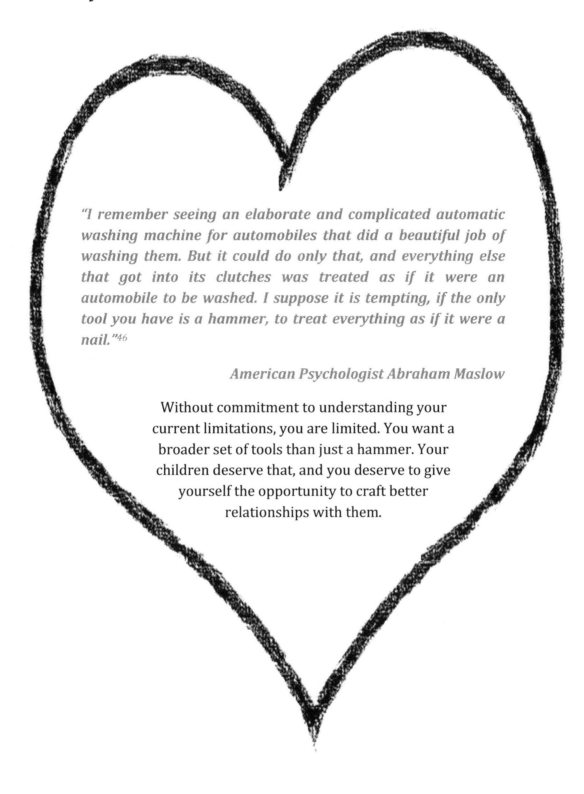

"I remember seeing an elaborate and complicated automatic washing machine for automobiles that did a beautiful job of washing them. But it could do only that, and everything else that got into its clutches was treated as if it were an automobile to be washed. I suppose it is tempting, if the only tool you have is a hammer, to treat everything as if it were a nail."[46]

American Psychologist Abraham Maslow

Without commitment to understanding your current limitations, you are limited. You want a broader set of tools than just a hammer. Your children deserve that, and you deserve to give yourself the opportunity to craft better relationships with them.

Flight Path: Stage 2

'Define Winning'

Stage 2: Set the Destination 'Define Winning'

The second stage of the flightpath is to set your destination by defining what winning is to you and your family. Winning can mean many things to many people. Let us just expand on that first and then you can figure out your own.

Winners

So what really defines a winner? In sports, it is usually the person or team with the most points on the scoreboard. It could be the fastest, the strongest, or the most creative. In business, it could be who makes the most money, who lasts the longest, or who sells the best products. Are you more of a winner if you win more than somebody else? How many times do you have to win to be a winner?

Think of two people you believe to be winners. Are they the same? Probably not, but I imagine they share similar characteristics in certain areas. Most winners are people who make best use of their potential under pressure. They take their circumstances and the various talents they have and find a way to deliver on things they set out to achieve. **Winners keep going and they know how to improve because they make improvements happen.**

With this comes a sense of fulfilment and a deep personal pride. Most of all, winners are those who find peace within themselves for the efforts they have made and the obstacles they have overcome. As they progress in life and grow into retirement, their ego stops needing to be fed by continued success in the arena they have won in; and rather than feeling the depression of loss and past glory, they can grow through new challenges and new experiences. They can let go as easily as they grasped onto their dreams in the first place. This is what a 'Winning Parent' can do.

Here are some important questions for you to reflect upon:

- **Who are the winners you admire most in life?**

- **What qualities do they possess?**

- **Are these qualities available for you to tap into?**

- **How would you define what winning is to your children?**

The allure of winning in sports competition

Winning is a fascinating concept. Personally, something I have always been afflicted with is my need to avoid failure and my need to win. Why does it feel so good to win, so bad to lose? Winning drives people to great states of motivation and emotion and is so alluring. When you watch somebody who wins when they really wanted to, they almost look possessed. They are just totally invaded and so overcome with emotions that their normal behavior stops as joy seems to flood every cell of their bodies. A deep instinctive sense of power and pride seems to emerge. A raw and instant sense of growth in self-worth and self-importance floods one's brain, even if just for minutes. On the flip side, losing seems to have the same strength, but the other way: An immediate dropping off of self-worth and self-status clouds the brain, resulting in negative feelings such as anger, dejection, and self-pity. You see this so vividly at the conclusion of sporting finals or penalty shoot-outs in soccer. One person experiencing their highest excitement in life, while their losing competitor never feeling as low and hollow.

"All very natural," some would say. "It's all connected to our instincts and natural selection." "Survival of the fittest," so to speak. There is an opinion that it can be specifically traced to evolutionary biology, where winners will survive and go on while losers will be eaten and become extinct. Consequently, it is natural for a human being to drive towards victory and to fear losing at anything. It applies today just as powerfully as ever, and we can't escape this mental programming, no matter how trivialized the battle. Quizzes, board games, cooking, who has more friends, who has collected more stuff, visited more places, chatted to more famous people, looks prettier, who has the higher paid job, bigger house, faster car, more expensive things, who is more intelligent, more religious, more spiritual, a better friend... and on the list goes... No matter how trivial the competition, no matter how unorganized, how unofficial or how subtle, winning and losing dominate our thinking and behavior. The trouble with believing this 'instinct' approach is that it is a fixed way of looking at the causes of our behaviors. It's like we have no control over how we react to life and its various challenges. In some ways, this excuses us from trying to adapt, and from changing our attitudes and behaviors to be more resourceful and progressive. We will get to this in much more depth later as we explore social learning viewpoints and how we can adapt our brains.

'WE' won!

Many times I have witnessed parents and coaches react to winning and losing as if they were out there playing themselves. The thinking possibly being; "If my son/daughter is a winner then I am too, not just a winner in sport but as a parent too". Coaches can be the same. It hardly needs mentioning that the same pattern applies to losing, and this is where the pressure and blame can come in. If you buy into the **high** of associated winning you can't get out of it when losing occurs. In some ways, getting hooked on winning is like making a pact with the Devil, and worse it becomes addictive. Soon you need your little protégés to have success just to keep the cravings at bay. A loss can feel much more destructive than it should. ***Wanting to win changes to needing to win*** *and failure must be avoided at all costs. This is new territory and it changes the definition of winning.*

Winning mentality and the cost of 'make or break!'

There is an extreme philosophy on how to develop sports stars: ***Throw fifty eggs at a wall, and one of them won't break.***

This concept is built on finding the one rare person who can handle the mighty stresses of a training regime, not unlike Special Forces selection. It clearly has some relevance in terms of the difficulty of dealing with the training load required to become a top professional athlete. Despite the relevance, the thing this 'make or break' philosophy creates is 49 broken people for every one survivor. Is this something we really want to create in society? I include this philosophy for three reasons:

Reason one: We aren't all tough especially when we are young, and there is an individual breaking point at any given time for any individual. So it is important to remember how much each individual needs stretching, which area needs developing, and when to back off.

Reason two: Who decides what a winning mentality is for each person? When you examine all the psychological profiles and skills research, there are upwards of 50 psychological and emotional skills that can be exhibited by winners. All have various profiles, and all come from unique backgrounds. You have someone like boxer Floyd Mayweather who always displayed confidence, showmanship, and self-belief from a very young age, but someone like World Champion boxer Carl Froch who admits:

> *"Although I am pretty confident nowadays, I wasn't always like that. My nerves and lack of confidence meant I used to box like absolute crap, especially for England."*[47]

It must be remembered that people mature at different rates at different stages of their lives and you never know when it can happen, so to write youngsters off mentally or to try to force the process into them is unfair and unlikely to work. That is not to say discipline and mental skills can't be encouraged and nurtured. This is something all those interviewed talk about later in the book.

Reason three: This philosophy is subtle, and it has started to grow and spread across global youth sports. I have termed it **'Professional Junior Syndrome'**.

Professional Junior Syndrome

YouTube clips and news reports of Tiger Woods' upbringing did not help the growth of what appears to be the rise of the professional youth athlete. Woods became the poster child for the archetypal professional kid, destined for the top from age three. Venus and Serena Williams' rise to the top of tennis under their father's guidance was a similar tale. Such stories combined with the rise of Dr. K. Anders Ericsson's '10,000 hour rule' of deliberate practice[48] that flooded talent development advice, and paved the way for the 'champion by design' outlook, are based upon the sentiment: ***"If we start you early enough, practice hard enough, and get you the best coaching, we can make you a champion."*** Of course there is truth to this approach; but at what cost? What of the stories of all the thousands of children that this system does not work for? What of the stories of those many world-class performers that only specialized very late in their youth and came nowhere near 10,000 hours of deliberate practice? Did every successful golfer take Tiger Wood's approach? No! Take two-time Masters Champion Bubba Watson as the most obvious contrast. In boxing, Olympic Super Heavyweight gold medal winner Anthony Joshua only discovered boxing at aged 16, yet Floyd Mayweather has been punching away since four years old.

In many countries, the more money and time the Governing Bodies seem to invest in structured youth development (champion by design), the less effective they seem to be in producing champion performers. This could be written off as just a bad financial investment, but many of these Governing Bodies still seem comfortable in wasting money as more seems to pour through their sports. It is not their investment that is the concern. It is the investment of thousands of hours of time and money by individual families sold on the idea that their child will become a successful professional athlete. It is also worrying for the children themselves who after being coerced into early adulthood can lose their natural zest for play, experimentation, and risk taking through sport. Simply put, many youngsters can lose their innocence too quickly, their youth, and worse still be left feeling like failures if they don't reach the heights only few do.

It is fair to suggest that for even those who go on to the top through the 'regimented route', it does not guarantee a happy and emotionally rounded adult existence. Andre Agassi's autobiography <u>Open</u>[49] is a window into such a world. In fact, numerous researchers suggest that passionate adherence to the type of frequent and intense training (which characterizes the '10,000 hour' deliberate practice framework) may increase the chances of youngsters overtraining, incurring overuse injuries, and becoming burnt-out at an early age. This is not to mention the fact that many young competitors could possibly sacrifice opportunities to interact with other youngsters and forge long-term friendships outside of sport.[50] In many ways, youngsters who specialize early in a sport could feel socially isolated in their formative years, or 'socially handcuffed' by their demanding training constraints. It is really important to take these issues into account before committing to any 'regimented route' to sporting excellence.

A wider definition of winning

Perspective - When your child was born, how important was it that the child always won at sport compared with how much he or she would enjoy life?

That previous question was my first tweet on my @winningparent account. It is probably my most important one too. It gets right to the heart of your values, in other words, what is important to you above all else?

Exercise: The sports wizard and three wishes

Thinking about your children now, imagine that you could bestow *three* gifts on them related to their experiences in sport. Which *three* from the following list would you request from the 'sports wizard' to guarantee?

- **You will have incredible skills and fitness that you can show off all your life.**

- **You will win lots of competitions all your life.**

- **You will always be happy as long as you play sports.**

- **You will specialize in one sport and become very good at it.**

- **You will always make many good friends and positive social groups through sport.**

- **Sport will keep you fit, healthy, and emotionally balanced for life.**

- **You will become professional at a sport and be well paid for it.**

- **You will always enjoy all types of sports and learn endless life lessons by doing so.**

- **You will become famous through sports, always appearing in the media and center of attention.**

- **Sport will always provide you with high self-esteem and life confidence.**

- You will always be admired by others for your sporting prowess.

- Sport will make you very financially rich.

- As long as you are involved in sports either playing or coaching, you will be a positive person who helps many in society.

Do you have any immediate reactions or new awareness?

Is this a different list than the one you would have chosen when they were born?

What are your top three goals for your child based on your answers?

Do these goals stay at the front of your mind?

A) Generally

B) At tournaments and during competition

So what is your definition of winning? Write it here below, and revisit it often, to remind yourself what is really important to you when you come under pressure or lose your way a little.

Case Study: An interview with 'Winning Parent' Basma Hassan El Shorbagy

Basma Hassan El Shorbagy is the mother of two boys, Mohamed and Marwan, who have both become world class sportsmen. Mohamed is currently ranked the world's number one player with Marwan not far behind. Both became world youth champions. Both have graduated from university with degrees, and both are very well-rounded young men. I wanted to interview Basma and introduce her to you in this book because I have been very aware of how much her sons love her and include her in their individual careers. Mohamed in particular publically acknowledges the importance of his mother and requests that she follow him all over the world in his quest to become the best player on the planet. *"She is the strongest person I have ever met in my life. No one can imagine the amount of pressure and work she has to take care of. She handles everything for me off court so I can perform the way I do on court."*

I was intrigued by this and decided to ask Basma if she would reveal some of her experiences, opinions, and strategies around her 'Winning Parent' philosophy. Thankfully she agreed to talk to me and over a four hour discussion she revealed some fascinating insights.

Interview

Me: Hello Basma. Your boys still use you as massive inspiration and involve you very much in their profession. How have you achieved that state because many young men want to be on their own or away from their parents?

Basma: *I believe HOME is the first step to breed healthy values of family, love, and strength from the start. My husband and I have a strong relationship, and the boys always had love and discipline from both of us which gives them strength. Love leads to inspiration. They want to play and win for their family; it's inspiring to them. They don't need much motivation because they have inspiration. Marwan and Mohamed are strong men and they are proud of me their mother and they like being with me. They are so strong they don't mind everybody knowing that their mother is still important to them. Many young boys don't have this courage. They are afraid to let love be on show, especially with their parents.* **Love** *is a big word, I think.*

Also, I am their friend. They can talk to me like a friend about anything in their lives. They know I am strong and they know I push their independence, but they know I am there for them whenever they want me as a mother, a friend, and an advisor. I know how to talk to them individually and they know they can trust me 100% with anything. They feel really confident in me. They are proud of me, and this means they listen to me properly. So they don't feel bad pressure from me, just support and direction. They know I want to push as they do, but it's not in a desperate, horrible way.

Me: Being a parent of two competitive and very successful young sportsmen, what have you learned most of all?

Basma: *I've learned that they are different characters and need to be treated differently. Not only that they need different things at different ages of their lives; they need different things from age to age. What Marwan needed when he was 12 is much different from what he needed at 16. An example is that when they were young Mohamed always played better when I went to support him and shout for him. Everybody knew that I was really important for Mohamed and that I had this big helpful effect. With Marwan I used to have a bad pressure effect. He would worry that he was making me nervous or upset if he lost. So I caused him pressure. I could feel it, I talked to him about it, and we let him be alone for a while. Because he loves me and didn't quite know himself, he would never have asked me not to come. That is big advice for parents; you need to understand your own effect on your children, what works best at the stage you're at. It is intelligence, and you* **feel** *it. When Marwan was a little older I had a good effect when I watched him and still do now. I know when he needs inspiration and when he needs quiet time.*

Me: What has been the hardest part?

Basma: *This is the most emotional question. Having two children competing in the same sport and doing well in their own right is good in many ways but really hard for me as a mother. I'm concerned about my giving them equal support and attention. I just want them to be very close as brothers because family is the most important thing. I want them to support each other and be there no matter what. Naturally they will want to beat each other when they play, but I never want them to put squash above their relationship. It is hard when they play each other, but we can't stop that.*

When one of them is down it is hard especially if the other one is up. All mothers will know this feeling; it's an instinct to protect them both. That is very hard, but we've done well as a family and my husband is brilliant at supporting us through that. He isn't as directly involved as I, but just as important. He is calm and gives good perspectives.

Me: What is your character and does it affect your children in their sport?

Basma: *My character is always to master one not many things at a time. I am very driven to accomplish what I want to achieve. So if I am going to do something, I am going to do it to my very best. I want to help my boys become champions because they want to be champions, and I take it very seriously. I have never had to tell them being the best is important. When we don't talk squash we are a normal family and do many other things. Squash will not be forever, and then I will put my mind to something else. When we do talk about squash and while Marwan and Mohamed are playing, we are very, very, committed to being the best.*

So I suppose I have provided a lot of drive to my boys, they perhaps see it in me, and because they respect me they want to do it for me and with me as well as by themselves. I am strong in myself too; maybe, they can't have their mother being stronger than them (laughs).

Me: Are there any particular values you set above all else? Maybe a motto you have?

Basma: *Not really a motto. Above all I want my sons to be good brothers, be there for each other, supportive, and never display any jealousy. I want them to be friends more than anything else. They are different characters so I don't want them to fall out because they see things differently. I want that to be a strength for them both.*

Also I learned a lot from Mohamed's first coach. He set a great mentality in us all. He said, "If you lose, you have to go back and work harder than before." This has been very important and helps after some of the low times.

Me: How do you deal with pressure before or during play? Do you have any coping mechanisms? Anything psychological, religious, or a type of mentor you think of?

Basma: *I get nervous and I think it is natural. I've seen you Danny with Laura; you know how hard it is. You just want it for them because how much* *they work. Some moments are harder, but I just try to stay as calm as I can. I think my boys need to see me being strong and calm, not being disappointed or looking sad. Just some deep breaths sometimes. It's hard.*

Generally, I just have to be strong for them. I must cope with both the highs and lows. Growing up I learned to keep away from the politics and not care what people said about me and how I worked with my sons. I kept them away from the politics. It was good training and makes me tough.

Me: What do you look for or value in a coach?

Basma: *The coach is most important in setting the psychology and giving new information that will make a champion. Not just any coach can convince me that they are a coach. A real coach is extremely important to my sons. A real coach gets to know Marwan or Mohamed well and affects them, not just offering information. They change them and influence them where they need it. Coaches set the mentality to be a champion, and it is very important they know what it takes to be a champion player, especially on the mental side.*

Mohamed's first coach was a past champion and – as I mentioned before - he said something that has always stuck with us which was "If you lose, go away and train harder." It's all about hard work and respecting opponents at the end of the match for their efforts.

I think coaches should be able to talk with parents, but also have lots of time on their own with the player. A coach who is a secure person and can see the parts where a parent can help is important. A good coach can teach parents their ideas and secrets too.

I don't think everyone is a great coach. Some do it for themselves and they don't have new ideas. Good coaches know what to do in pressure situations. They have been through it maybe; they know what it takes to be a champion. They understand the ups and downs and how to get through them to become the best.

Me: How do you keep the relationship with the coaches?

Basma: *When my boys were much younger I was involved a lot more. Mohamed's first coach got me involved in the sessions all the time. He had me timing things, measuring footwork, answering problems, and discussing things together. He taught me many secrets of being a champion squash player and gave me confidence that I could learn the game (I had never* *played squash). He told Mohamed to listen to me because he thought I was intelligent and that I could help him. So we all really worked together, and that was really important for us.*

*As the boys got older they saw coaches on their own more and then to keep me updated told me things they had been working on. Their coaches considered it important to involve me because the boys wanted me involved. **That is the main point; they wanted me; I didn't have to force it.** I make sure I thank the coaches a lot and let them know we appreciate them. It's not easy to find a good coach; so when you find one it's important to let them know I appreciate them. They are helping my boys as people not just the squash playing.*

Me: Have you got any advice? Do you see things going on that parents can improve?

Basma: *I see children being forced into sports that they don't have neither the natural talent or love for. So when you watch your child, I think you need to try and think with your head, not your heart. You need to be logical. Some children just aren't going to reach the professional level, yet many parents are disappointed in them for this.*

I see parents comparing their children to others. I think this is bad; I think it causes bad pressure and bad feelings. Competition is an important element of life, but maybe it's better to educate children to strive for self-improvement rather than making comparisons with other children. I also notice how some parents push, push, and push with no rest, many hours each day. They force children into very long spells of training. Children have lots of energy but get tired very quickly; they need good rest. The best parents talk of rest and sometimes stop their children competing to get rest.

Both parents need to be a solid team. The family needs to be strong. Strong families really help, especially around all the politics that happen in youth sports. Lots of damaging things can be said and done, and the children need protecting a bit from it all, and not get involved in all the adult politics, especially when they're young.

Me: How much would you credit yourself in your boys' development?

Basma: I have helped from a distance and think of myself as support for them. I am their friend; they can both trust me and I trust them. My biggest hopes are that they are two good men who are happy in their lives and keep looking out for each other. If that happens (which I think it has so far), then both myself and my husband can say we did a good job.

Reflections: Before I give you my reflections on the interview, what has impacted you here? What is the main thing you will take notice of from Basma?

My Reflections

Speaking with Basma was first and foremost enjoyable, and I could chat for another four hours with her. Her fascinating and enthusiastic responses to some soul-searching questions made for a wonderful conversation, and I felt privileged to hear many of her thoughts and stories. It was therapeutic to share some experiences we've both had supporting our loved ones from close quarters at the pinnacle of the professional squash world. Basma's clarity of philosophy was amazing, and this is why she answered my questions so quickly and thoroughly. It was as if she'd asked these questions of herself a hundred times before. I sensed massive confidence, humility, and determination from this lady, and it is no surprise that her two sons are excelling in their lives. Nor was it surprising to meet someone who appears happy with her own life, which after all is healthy and wonderful.

What did I learn?

I resonated with many aspects of what Basma said, in particular the point about the need to be a constant and steady strong character in the background, especially among the politics and underground criticism thrown your way when you are closely involved with loved ones in sport. The ability to rise above the external distractions, and maintain unwavering love and support is the true hallmark of the 'Winning Parent'. I have noticed that Judy Murray, the mother of tennis champion Andy, demonstrates this quality on a consistent basis.

I learned that it is possible to be a 'Winning Parent' in all the ways you personally define winning. Basma wants her children to be champions. Her drive and vision for this is strong and she is not afraid to admit it. Basma wants her sons to be ranked number one and two in the world and play the world championship final together, as the Williams sisters achieved in tennis. I really admire this courage, and I think where the pedigree exists, then it is good for a parent to be a driving force. Basma was aware of this key point and pointed out that this strategy would be dangerous to follow if the background pedigree of the player wasn't there. As she alluded to in the interview, many parents fall into the trap of believing their child will become a champion in a certain sport, in spite of the fact that they don't necessarily have the pedigree or genetic make-up to excel. It is important that coaches and parents have a realistic outlook in this sense, even though it is difficult to predict the future. However, in Basma's case, both Marwan and Mohamed displayed standout ability at a young age and became multiple world level junior champions, so she sees no reason not to go for maximum ambition.

Through the entire interview the two words that I kept thinking were **love** and **support**. A special strong bond within the family was obvious. I believe that is where the secret of the 'Winning Parent' philosophy lies. For Basma, it would not be 'win at all costs'. More important is brotherly love, family bond, and personal happiness. Success in life for her sons certainly includes becoming champion sports players but would count for nothing if they were miserable, spiteful, or unhappy. It appears that one of Basma's objectives is to help shape rounded, well-balanced, individuals who will make a positive contribution to society, and likewise to nurture individuals who are comfortable in expressing the love and bond they have with their family members. For herself, it seemed that winning is in committing to help support her family by exuding personal strength and having faith that her intuitions and vision will lead to success on and off the squash court. As if squash just happens to be the temporary vehicle that can teach her sons how to be champions of life.

Lastly, it was clear that Basma was aware that her two sons are different characters, different personalities. While certain methods worked for one, the same methods didn't necessarily have the same impact for the other son. Adapting her approach to meet each of her sons' requirements is one of Basma's toughest challenges, but necessary to work on.

Summary

Alignment with your children is the most important thing in respect to your definition of winning. You all have equal contributions to make to the decision and must get to a point *where you know you are on the same page.* Begin the process of coming up with your own definition of winning by reflecting on what is really important to you as a parent. Talk with your child and lay down your *shared* and *agreed* understanding of what winning means. Understand that this is the destination, and it is the most important thing above all else. Maybe rank your areas of winning in a list, or write it down in some form of motto or statement. Be sure to revisit this definition every so often to check that any of you haven't lost sight of the destination. You do not want to drift off to other destinations.

Keep your course strong. When times change, as they will, have another conversation with your children and reset your definition of winning.

Notes & Reminders

Flight Path: Stage 3

'Educate Yourself'

Stage 3: Fuel up 'Educate Yourself'

"Human history becomes more and more a race between education and catastrophe."[51]

H. G. Wells.

The third stage of the flightpath is **fueling-up**. In order to make sure you can make your journey as fruitful as possible, you need to keep putting fuel into the tank. Fuel in this sense is **education** and **knowledge**, and hopefully this will lead to personal *wisdom*.

Knowledge and Wisdom

By educating yourself you will acquire knowledge; by applying that knowledge over time you will build wisdom. Knowledge shared around like currency is quite easy to obtain, if you know where to look for it. Knowledge can be amassed in huge amounts in the traditional form of books, documents, libraries, and teachings. While a **knowledgeable** person may know *what* to apply to a problem, the **wise** person is strong at knowing *when, where, and how much* to apply their influence. With matters of relationships and sports coaching, in this case parenting, wise people tend to be able to take on new knowledge with the overall understanding that **'it depends'**.

BE CAREFUL – BEWARE OF THE FUNDAMENTALIST

Be aware of anyone preaching to you that they have the only and complete answer to your problems. It may have worked for them in their context and naturally they will be convinced they have found THE answer to a problem they had, but that does not necessarily mean it is the answer to yours. As they try to shoehorn their theories into your life situation be alert for defensiveness and subsequent attacks if you do not follow their wisdom. If they insist and will not stop trying to convince you, then be even more wary!

Likely fundamentalists: Desperate coaches, perfect parents, defensive academics, self-promoting experts, and know it all's!

The ultra-runner and author of <u>Ultramarathon Man</u>[52] Dean Karnazes encapsulates the point articulated above very well. Discussing the issue of being quizzed by people about his training methods, nutritional intake, or racing strategies, Karnazes responded with some thoughtful and insightful information:

"I'm quick to preface my answers by letting the advice-seeker know that what works best for me may not work best for him or her. I always encourage people to try new things and experiment to find out what works best for them. Listen to everyone, follow no-one!"[53]

Wisdom is the goal because wisdom is the product of well applied knowledge. I really enjoy how popular British journalist Miles Kington explained the difference between knowledge and wisdom: **"Knowledge is *knowing* that *a tomato is a fruit*; *wisdom is* not putting it in a fruit salad."**[54]

Wisdom is earned through experience and usually involves memorable life lessons. Over time, doses of pain and moments of joy become the teacher, enabling a person to understand the complications of real life and how to move past them.

In parenting, as time passes, you are able to deal with situations more wisely not just because of your extra knowledge but because of how you have applied that knowledge and what results came from it in your real situation. In sport, you may be given the knowledge that shouting at your child creates pressure on them; yet in reality you have learned that occasionally when the time is right, expressing your anger and disappointment helps the situation.

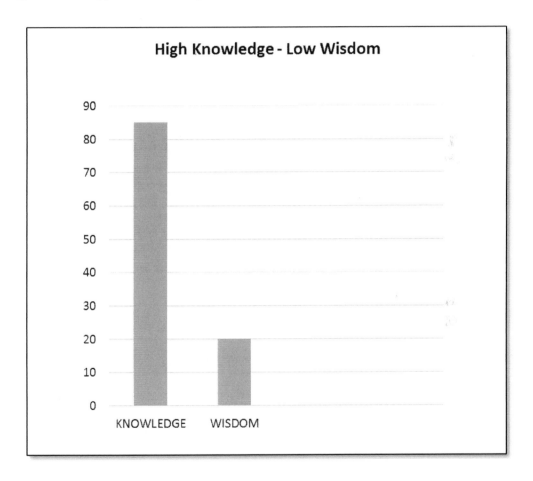

A common state of affairs with many of us, particularly in new experiences is that we have acquired the knowledge, but don't necessarily have the wisdom to utilize the knowledge effectively.

Knowledge and Wisdom over time

QUANTITY

TIME

KNOWLEDGE — ◆ — WISDOM

This graph illustrates the typical pathways of how wisdom usually follows knowledge. It can take time to get to the point where wisdom overtakes your knowledge, years in fact. Both pathways need to be worked at and appreciated for how they are different from each other. It's hard to put a wise head on young shoulders.

Knowing the difference here may help you deal with your teenage 'know it all's'. Yes, they have knowledge about new things and can certainly beat you with the latest information on matters. In this way you are a little behind them; but in the overall wisdom stakes, you are most probably ahead. This wisdom should allow you not to react to their jibes and opinions. You should be able to clearly notice that the way they act (as if they know it all) is actually just their need to show they are clever, which in itself, is not true. Yet they must learn the difference themselves. Rather than put them down for this and point out their naivety, allow them their youth and innocence. One day they will figure it out and know the difference. Personally, I hit these realizations to this day, and they are very humbling.

Read these example statements and in your experience consider if they are true or false?

- *Training with weights will improve your chances of gaining more speed.*
- *Reducing telling off young competitors when they lose will help them in the long-term.*
- *Focusing on your performance leads to better performances than focusing on results.*
- *The more you practice, the better you will get.*

- *Publicizing how well your daughter is doing will create too much pressure on her.*
- *More coaching will lead to more improvement.*
- *Fitness tests prove how fit you are.*
- *That a professional player is being successful is most likely the result of very good sports parenting when they were young.*
- *Having the best sports kit gives you the best chance of winning.*
- *Being angry at a child has more impact than remaining calm with them.*

If you want to know if you scored correctly the answers are on page 999..!

The point here is that you were asked to reflect upon your experience so how you can be wrong all depends!

Here is a different question: According to the latest scientific research compiled from over 100 universities from across the world, which of the following do you think are true?

1. *The trap we walk into is when we tend to think there is one truth in the world; a fragment that is true for all people at all times, in all cultures through the whole of history. There is only one perspective: Your perspective.*

2. *"Until lions have their historians, tales of the hunt shall always glorify the hunter."*

3. *Everybody is right says Ken. True, but only partially!*

4. *Parent:* *"I am right, listen to me."*
   Child: *"No you're not I am! You don't understand."*
   Parent: *"I do understand but the truth on this occasion is..."*

Think of situations you have with your children or others for that matter. Those situations where you believe that you are 100% correct and **they** are 100% wrong. What happens?

Ken Wilber is one of the world's most eminent and published philosophers. One of his really interesting suggestions is that nobody can be completely right or completely wrong; everyone is correct at some level. Wilber says:

"I have one major rule: Everybody is right. More specifically, everybody — including me — has some important pieces of truth, and all of those pieces need to be honored, cherished, and included in a more gracious, spacious, and compassionate embrace. To Freudians, I say, "Have you looked at Buddhism?" To Buddhists, I say, "Have you studied Freud?" To liberals, I say, "Have you thought about how important some conservative ideas are?" To conservatives, I say, "Can you perhaps include a more liberal perspective?" And so on, and so on, and so on... At no point have I ever said, "Freud is wrong, Buddha is wrong, Liberals are wrong, Conservatives are wrong." I have only suggested that they are true but partial. And on my own tombstone, I dearly hope that someday they will write: "He was true but partial."[55]

So as you go about collecting knowledge, please remember Ken Wilber's viewpoint that any information you are taking is only part of the truth. Good scientists know this, and so do good priests. A 'Winning Parent' will know this too as they go about evaluating their children's sports performances from a less rigid standpoint.

Choose the best knowledge for you and the appropriate dose!

Now don't get me (or Ken) wrong here: Not all knowledge is equal! Some knowledge is better than others. For example, I would prefer an engineer to build my hot air balloon, but not a physician. I know who I want to help me with my altitude sickness! I also want the engineer to be the best one I can find at putting together hot air balloons, not cars. I want somebody who has experience and a proven track record of safety and effectiveness. If I was looking to travel fast and far, I would need the services of an engineer who specialized in speed, endurance, and safety. The more specific my needs, the more detailed expertise I require. This is the same with you and your sports parenting requirements. So find the appropriate type of education that suits your situation best. Nothing too weak. Nothing too powerful.

We all have the capacity for different **amounts** of knowledge too before we overflow. Some of us simply have bigger tanks to fill and can quite easily digest large volumes of information. Understanding yourself and how much information is best for you to take in is a key self-awareness skill. A fuel tank that is overflowing into the engine will be just as problematic as one with no fuel at all – you will go nowhere! Topping yourself up at the right times depends on your pace and your efficiency. So again, how you use your knowledge and at what speed you can process it will determine how much you need. Smoother journeys tend to require less topping up as opposed to those stop and start rides that can be exciting, yet more demanding.

Your fueling options

There are many ways to acquire knowledge, and we all have our preferred means. Here you have chosen a book to gather information and it may be all you feel you need, but there are so many other ways to fuel up your brain.

Tree of knowledge

Questions for reflection:

- **What methods of gaining knowledge have worked best for you in your life so far?**

- **Which ones may be of new value to you if you tried them out more often?**

- **Let's go through some of the best ways of fueling up:**

The Power of Books

For me, books have been a great source of knowledge and investment. Despite gaining a degree when I was 22 years old, I only really started digesting books for educational purposes about four years later. Of course, I had used books in my formal education, but rarely did so out of pure interest and the desire to educate myself. Looking back, this was rather strange because as you will read below it was a small book that set me on my path back in 1990 and gave me the fuel to really push forward.

1990 – How a book changed the course of my life!

I embarked on a rare visit to our small college library and headed for the psychology section. I couldn't make sense of anything I looked at: Thick textbooks and endless pages of writing, where would I start with that? Then I went to the sports section where I found a small yellow book under the 'sport psychology' heading, the book was called <u>The Inner Game of Tennis</u>[56] by Timothy Gallwey. It changed the course of my life.

I had heard about sport psychology through watching a TV documentary on some of the best Olympians, mainly Daley Thompson the Olympic Decathlon Gold medalist and British national hero. *"It's 90 percent in the mind. I am the greatest out there, I am a born winner,"* Daley would spout. He would also ask, *"Who is the greatest athlete in the world?"* - Before declaring with a beaming smile, *"You're looking at him."*

In the book, I found interesting phrases and ideas about visualization, mood states, dealing with anxiety, and using positive self-talk. The main part was how we had two parts to us, which Gallwey called **Self-One** and **Self-Two**[57], one critical and corrective, the other more flowing and free. "I knew it", I thought. "I knew you could train your brain; I knew there was something important about that voice in my head. I can affect myself. I can improve my confidence and do more than I think I can. It can help me play better at sports. Maybe I have been holding myself back without knowing it." So I borrowed the book from the library; my first ever in fact outside of school. I had three weeks to return it, but could renew it if I took it back to be stamped, which I did many times. So important, so useful in helping me to improve my circumstances, I couldn't stop returning to the library to have it stamped. I simply couldn't live without it at that time.

It started with self-awareness, then practice...

Through self-awareness brought on by my circumstances, my reflections, and the education Mr. Gallwey gave me, I had the tools to move onwards and upwards. The self-help boom had not really taken off by 1990, yet I learned through catching my brain's thinking habits and then practicing changing some of those thoughts; my mental health improved tremendously. Nowadays they call it emotional intelligence, cognitive behavioral therapy, a growth mindset or mindfulness, but basically I got better control of my brain. Of course, I was still naïve, did stupid things, and stayed young and foolish; but my self-esteem and optimism for my future took a sharp rise. I believe my whole personality grew and to this day I take great strength through knowing that when I was a young person I independently found a way to build huge personal and professional success. I know I could have quite easily gone the other way. There is no doubt Mr. Gallwey's book helped me.

The wonderful thing about books is that they are easy to get hold of and provide massive value for what you pay. I always think that if I just get one piece of helpful information that improves my situation even just one time, then it is worth it. Anything more is just bonus time.

Interviews, conversations, and chats

Talking to people and asking questions, whether you chat over coffee or do it more formally, is a brilliant way of building up your fuel tank of education. If you pick interesting people who have passion and enthusiasm, they cannot help answering your questions. They will equally enjoy the sharing of ideas and questioning that arise. They know that it helps them and makes them feel good, and they also know they are helping you, which is a marvelous feeling.

Researching for **The Winning Parent** has in itself been a powerful learning experience for me. In particular, I gained huge knowledge from the many interviews and conversations I have had. Talking and listening with people one respects is valuable for gaining knowledge and wisdom. It has become apparent to me that the hours I have spent philosophizing, deliberating, and dissecting particular developmental issues with people I have respect and admiration for – has been as equally enlightening as the many hours I have spent in classrooms. The value of learning in this manner should never be discounted or underestimated.

If you have improved your level of *self-awareness* after reading **Stage 1** of the flightpath and *defined winning* from **Stage 2**, then you can really focus on areas in interviews that apply to you.

Exercise: Have a go at reading this interview provided below; and afterwards write down anything that resonated with you or made you reflect strongly on your personal situation.

An interview with David Pearson

David Pearson has been a coach for 35 years. He is a father of four; two daughters and two sons. David was the longest serving Head National Coach across all sports in the United Kingdom from 1995 until 2010. David has coached four world champion squash players: two women, two men – coincidence!? Widely acknowledged as one of the best Squash Coaches in the world, 'DP' as he is fondly known, continues to coach all players across the playing standard spectrum and from all corners of the globe. Winner of UK Sports 'Mussabini Medal' for outstanding coaching in 2000, DP is renowned for two special coaching skills. First, his technical knowledge and ability to get his players to learn and apply new technical skills. Second, his ability to form strong and lasting relationships with players by focusing as much on the person before him as on the player aspect of their make-up. The volume of young players he has seen come and go in his 35 year journey gives him a unique insight into aspects he feels has made the difference to those who have done well in the sport but more important than that, who have enjoyed happy and fulfilled lives. He remains a life coach to many people who have been lucky to experience his tutelage, mentorship, and friendship.

Me: You refer to the word 'background' when it comes to discussing players and their parents. What exactly do you mean by this?

David: *To me the word 'background' has emerged as my word for the foundations and upbringing that performers went through as a children. What values were instilled into them from their upbringing? Things like schooling, the place they lived, and the people they were involved with, the* *rules that were set – that kind of thing. I believe the biggest part of it is how the parents 'parented' for want of a better phrase. If parents provide support and enough love so their children feel secure (yet their children are still challenged and given room for their natural personality to flourish), then their children will become more emotionally stable as they grow up. Children need boundaries and love, but also need space to be themselves, to grow into what they really are as individuals. You can't control that.*

I don't believe children want sympathy or too much interference in their adventures, I just think they want clear boundaries set and clear rules set about standards of behavior. Only when **bad behavior** *occurs should the parent step in.*

You can easily recognize the children who have learned what it is to respect people. They have calmness about them around adults and speak to their parents normally and respectfully. They aren't scared, just polite and confident. You can tell they have been given a voice within the family household, yet they haven't taken this too far and become too cocky or condescending. If they come for coaching and I ask them questions they are comfortable having a debate or suggesting their opinions, and the mother or father doesn't jump in trying to talk for them.

I think later on when they get to the late teens and in to adulthood, 'the breakout years' as I say, that is when the effects of the background are really noticed. Players really need to show independent qualities and life starts to hit them a bit more head on. If they haven't got that deep sense of security then all sorts of problems can start. Not really bad things you'd notice, but just subtle things like how they deal with setbacks or how they talk to people who deserve a bit of respect, even adults or younger children.

Blame and the need to mature early

A common theme is when people blame others when things go wrong. With a good background, they get to work themselves and fix the problem without much fuss. With a bad background, all the excuses start! You start feeling the dishonesty and the subtle lying, stories they tell you don't always stack up, and you just lose trust in what they are telling you. It is an insecurity expressed as over-confidence and too much talk. When it comes down to it; they struggle to keep promises and consistently produce results. Then as a coach trying to help them, you are battling this deep insecurity and lack of maturity at the very time it is required the most. In sport you can't really wait until your 30's to mature because your body has slowed down. So those that do well and come through usually show great maturity and self-assuredness as they came out of their teenage years.

I have noticed the way Jordan Spieth has been dealing with success in golf. Even at 21, you can tell if someone has a good background. He talks of his younger sister's inspiration a lot, his parents don't over-react when he wins, and he doesn't over-react either! He has a really healthy perspective of what winning means, and he behaves naturally. Maybe this was why he remained so composed to win the Masters tournament in 2015.

Humility

Remaining humble and keeping your feet on the ground is another major part of the journey of sport. If they as children have valued winning too highly, then it all becomes too much when they're older. The ego feels too inflated, and again you see lots of things in a person in how they react to winning as much as how they react to losing. Of course it's always better to win than to lose, as that is the nature of life I suppose. It's what we all work and strive for, but how you handle it and how it affects you, and what it teaches you is the most important part. There are plenty of superstars – people like Roger Federer, Sachin Tendulkar, and Jack Nicklaus – who have managed success and attention well. They are champions of both life and of sport.

Me: So are you suggesting that without the correct background people can't turn it around?

David: No not at all. I just think it is far more unlikely if they haven't been reared with boundaries and security. It can be a two way street as well, and this is really important.

Me: What exactly do you mean?

David: Lots of good things can come out of adversity also. I've seen kids who come out of really challenging upbringings become hard and tough. They do well in spite of their parents who may have been nasty or unloving. They have a point to prove and have gone down the positive reaction path rather than the destructive one. Rather than rebelling, something in them fired up, and they got on a mission never to feel like that again. They take control of their own lives and don't just give up or be a victim. I have had a world *champion player like that, who took a really tough upbringing and turned it positive through determination and incredible toughness. Saying all that, the issues from childhood still affect people all their lives; and despite going on to be successful in sport, there can be lingering personal problems and resentment. So it is really very complicated. You do see winners like this who have really deep personal issues and self-identity problems; and I suppose this is where the coach sometimes takes on a father/mother figure role. That is where coaching goes deeper than just the sport, and is why all the great coaches are coaches of people first, not just players.*

Me: In your experience, what is the most repeated mistake parents make with their young competitors?

David: *It's all about the winning. If you don't win, it's the end of the world, causing too much emotion and over-analysis. It takes the fun out of it for the kids. The parents can't appreciate the process and journey and all the different phases that kids go through. Some children don't mature till later on, and that's from physical and maturational perspectives. A coach who is any good will take the child through a longer path to improvement, keeping it light, and taking winning and losing as part of that path. So parents need to reinforce this; yet many now get caught up in the rankings and trophies.*

All the youth players I have seen playing who win generally win because they're just good! Later on in the upper age group things can change with more effort and training; but when they're little they just need to be left to play. If they're going to win, then they're going to win not because the parent forces it or comes up with master plans etc.

Another problem I see is that many parents can only talk about their own child. "My Sarah this, My Sarah that..." The conversations aren't normal; it always ends up back on their child. The funny thing is that they don't know they are doing it. This kind of obsession is too much, and I've rarely seen any good come from it. The child dominates the mind of the parent so much that they can't see the good in others and how it's not all about them.

Me: What are some of the worst examples of sports parenting you've noticed?

David: *I've seen a few cases of mental abuse which was horrific. Negative comments, personal blame, public telling offs, and drunken outbursts.*

Blaming the other parent for the child's failings such as: "You're just like your stupid mother, no wonder she left us." This consistently results in a slow erosion of the child's ability to have fun with the sport. It's terrible really.

Another common example is when parents see their child as an asset. The child achieves short-term success, and the parent feels great about this situation; and they are quick to inform everyone about their child's accomplishment. But sometimes it goes beyond normal pride of your children. It becomes about their status within the community and not the child's.

Me: Have you noticed any damaging long-term effects on players and family?

David: *I think if winning is over-celebrated in youth sport, it can lead to the youngsters being given too much status too early. I suppose it's the 'big fish in a small pond' scenario. When they climb up to the higher levels of their sport it can be quite a sharp drop in status because it is so much more difficult to win. In fact, this is possibly where most people get it wrong. In most sports the successful transition from high performing youth players to senior is remarkably difficult. Only very few do it quickly and smoothly. You get this drop in status for the players, their family, and coach. Suddenly they aren't winning or seemingly performing as well as they used to. Therefore, blame starts to creep in, and pressure keeps building. If you're not careful during this critical phase, players can give up purely because of the feelings of inadequacy and drop in ego. This is where the best parents stand by the longer process and douse the flames of panic and blame. These are the times when you really can tell how the youngster has been raised and if they've been spoiled or controlled too much. They need to understand that things take hard work and life is a journey full of ups and downs; and it's hard to get this as a young player who has always had their parents bailing him or her out.*

Me: Have you been able to challenge parental behavior that you understand to be limiting, or damaging? If so, how have you approached it?

David: *Yes, I have stepped in if I see things going really bad or if parents have asked me what I think. I have mostly done this through casual conversations and used stories or past examples, and highlighted behavior that I consider unacceptable. I don't think you can ever do it as if you are telling them off; it is a hard job after all. Sometimes I have found that all that* *is needed is a little prompt or idea helping them to see it a different way, and that can help.*

Me: Do you think it is part of a coach's responsibility or duty to coach parents as part of the process of youth sport development?

David: *No I don't see it that way. The parents need to bring with them a level of awareness to begin with and not be too involved and pushy. They need to know the actual effects they have on their children before a coach can contribute a few ideas. If they know this, you can casually talk to them on a **logical** level, not an **emotional** one. This is linked to the background I mentioned earlier. Parents who have had a good background and are quite secure in themselves and wise are much easier to have logical conversations with.*

Me: Yes, I think this is a crucial point you make. You worked with your own daughter for many years as a junior and professional performer. What was difficult about this? What did this experience teach you?

David: *The only difficult thing was watching her compete. When she competed, I was emotionally too high and couldn't enjoy the match. I would be a bit nervous. It was a strange feeling. It taught me that I had to calm down or not watch her play because it became off-putting for her. I also gained a valuable lesson sat with you once, Danny. You were watching Laura and I was sitting next to you helping and listening to you and all your fidgeting and stress. I thought, "Wow, is that what I am like when I watch Jenny, my daughter?"*

Me: I remember that well, yes. It was a big learning moment for me too, hearing you admit that. It made me see that I was too involved and needed to back off. I suppose that is what is good about working with other people. Parents could learn lots from other parents by sharing experiences and helping each other. Did it give you empathy for other parents? Did it change your coaching approach with other parents at all?

David: *Oh, yes it did! I was able to realize the type of things parents felt. It explained a lot of what I had seen as their weird behavior. I immediately adopted more empathy and was less harsh on them in my own mind, which probably came across much better. I would also tell the children to be nicer to their parents because I had been on the other side and knew that a kind word of appreciation made a huge difference in settling me down as a father.*

Me: What have the best parents been generally good at when working with you?

David: *Those parents who turn up, drop off their children, and leave the coach to the coaching. Then when invited in by either the coach or the player they can show a genuine interest and can listen without forcing their opinions. Generally the best parents are quite simple and uncomplicated people. They introduce their kids to the sport, enjoy watching them play and learn, introduce them to good coaches, and help out if asked. When they start to show promise and even win a few things,* **they stay exactly the same**, *apart from providing more support in time and money where it is needed.*

Me: What coaching qualities do you think a parent should look for in a potential coach for their children?

David: These qualities are what I believe are most important in a coach:

Passion - You want a coach who sees coaching as a vocation not a job or simple money earner. They have to look like they love coaching, even if they never got paid for it.

Relationship skill - They have to be good at getting along with different people and being friendly and showing strong leadership. The coach must be consistent no matter what standard of performer they work with. You want them giving their professional best every time a player requests it.

Artistic and open minded - You want to see creative ideas and somebody who moves with the times. They will have good foundations but be able to keep up to date with how the sport changes and how it may look in the future.

Relaxed and non-controlling - You need to sense maturity in the coach in that they can laugh and have fun and sometimes admit when they're wrong. They should generally encourage the players to work with other experts not just them. You don't want a bully who sulks and shouts when they don't get what they want.

Educational and interesting - You want your child gaining educational factors related to life and general knowledge. And you want a coach that asks questions not just about the sport or technique but about the child's opinions on other issues too.

Fun and humor - A good coach should somehow be able to bring laughter to the sessions. Poking fun, self-depreciation, or telling funny stories shows that the coach will be good at relaxing young people, and that is when they learn at their best. A sports performer's journey is so unchartered, full of ups and downs, hopes and fears, on the edge of frustration, always striving for improvement, while others are trying to beat them down. Having a good sense of humor and people around you who keep perspective can relax you through all these times is very important.

What did you learn here? Write down below what you took as valuable to you:

As a guide I have shown you what struck a chord with me and what I learned.

Clear boundaries, not controlling

What was refreshing speaking with David was that he hasn't become bogged down in some of the modern terms and literature regarding parenting and sports. He is not trying to prove or disprove anything, just speaking his mind as he sees it. In many ways DP is a throwback coach and his views on sports parenting spring directly from personal experiences. His explanation of the background is a refreshingly simple way of summing up the **nature** and **nurture** debate. I really liked his assertion: "Children need boundaries and love but also need space to be themselves, to grow into what they really are as individuals. You can't control that."

A father himself, he does not infer that this is an easy thing to achieve or that he has been successful at it himself, but he does have a clear philosophy which he tries to stick to.

Winning in life – I thought that David Pearson viewed winning in life as more important than merely winning in the sports arena. The type of question David would ask is, "How can you be a winner if you cannot be a good person?" In his sports coaching, David believes very much that if you work on getting the solid basics of movement and rhythm, the rest will open up naturally, and this is exactly how he sees the role of parenting. Provide him with a well-rounded, responsible, and respectful person who has independent thinking qualities, and there is a chance that player can deal with improvement and competition at higher levels. If the person arrives unsure, unable to think for themselves, and too desperate for success, there will be significant problems, not just in progressing in sport, but in dealing with life.

Big picture - The concept of the journey or process kept cropping up all through our conversation. He had empathy for parents who often panicked too much about today's performances and results in youth sport. He understood that it's hard to step back and see the big picture, but he said it is vital that parents can do this.

Some children are just simply good - I found the point about players being 'just good' very interesting. Personally, I see an age when we believe everything can be achieved by design, when everyone can be made good or turned into a champion, and I believe this can put a lot of pressure on youngsters due to unrealistic expectations. David reminded us that some children are simply good at sport just because they are. Not everything can be explained when it comes to talent, sport, or indeed parenting and growing up. We can't blame ourselves for everything. That level of responsibility can become too much and cause levels of stress that prevent us from being the person we really need to be.

Fun and humor - Finally, I learned a simple but hugely important thing that David exudes himself and believes must be present: Fun and a good sense of humor. I know from other research and personal experiences that most people learn best, work best, and live best when they feel good about themselves and are stress free. Making things light and fun is clever when striving for achievements through a process of committed effort and sacrifice. The use of humor is therefore a huge help with this.

5 tips for effective educational chats

1. *Choose passionate and enthusiastic people to talk with who are on (or just above) your level. If they are too deep or to shallow for you, it will not work.*

2. **Compliment them first and then ask a question. This shows you are happy to elevate the child into a position of intellect relative to you on this subject.**

3. **Find a good time to talk – e.g. arrange a meeting or a coffee, or go for a few beers/wines.**

4. **Let them answer your questions. Don't butt in with all your own theories and ideas unless asked your opinion. They are the experts here - that is why you approached them.**

5. **Give their knowledge and advice a try. Most people ask for advice and listen but then fail to give it chance to work. See their advice through over time, and give it a chance to kick in.**

Learn from the coaches

The coaches themselves are a great source of knowledge. They should be able to offer you insights and information regarding issues you are interested in finding out more about. For example, if you have an interest in fitness they can be an excellent source of the sport-specific fitness demands and training methods for the sport they coach.

Dr. Anne Pankhurst, Education Consultant to the Professional Tennis Registry and previously the Coach Education Director for the Lawn Tennis Association commented:

"Parents generally want to know what competition their child is up against, how much, and what sort of practice they need to do and more generally, what their job is in enabling the development of their child. Most coaches tend to assume parents have a pre-existing knowledge of what this is, when of course why would they? It's this focus that needs to change so that the coach can help the parents to play a more supportive role in the whole process."[58]

BE CAREFUL

Parents sometimes want to know what competition their child is up against in order to assess whether that level of challenge meets the child's progressive needs. And it is great when parents do this; it should certainly be commended and

embraced. However, throughout my coaching experiences, some parents wish to ascertain what level of competition their child is encountering for self-gratification purposes. They want to establish their child`s chances of being victorious that given day, as 'winning' inflates their ego in the short-term; it provides the 'winning fix' they are seeking. Always be mindful that sometimes your desires are not aligned with your child's objectives. You may feel an ego boost after certain 'little victories', but what benefit is this to your child if they are unhappy, or being given a false sense of performance standard?

Personally speaking, I have always seen that part of a coach's job is to help parents with any questions they have about understanding the sport more or what my rationale is for the way I coach. A genuine question will always be answered to my best ability and I will go as far as recommending further reading or involving them in the session themselves. On occasion, I have taken parents on court and trained them what we are doing so they can get a practical feel of what they want to know. This has the added bonus of creating fun and of course building a shared understanding between us. It can be time consuming for me, but I know it has been of great value to parents to learn directly from me as well as from other sources.

So get out there and find those coaches who can help you understand more about your child's sport and their particular needs, strengths, and development ideas.

Intuition - Don't forget to learn from yourself

"The intuitive mind is a sacred gift and the rational mind is a faithful servant. We have created a society that honours the servant and forgotten the gift."[59]

Albert Einstein

Chances are you know your children extremely well, and on certain occasions it is important that you **trust** your feelings as opposed to your thoughts. Have confidence in your own intuition. This requires a lot of trust in yourself. Going for walks or taking long showers and thinking things through can give room for your own ideas to emerge.

These ideas can be just as powerful as any expert opinion coming in. Trusting your 'gut instinct' is not always the best thing to rely on but it can be great too.

Malcolm Gladwell's excellent book <u>Blink: The Power of Thinking without Thinking</u>[60] provides a super set of examples and stories where intuition rules.

Trusting your intuition does not mean barging in with your opinions all the time in highly emotional states, it simply means taking the course of action that feels right to you. Intuition works best when you have had a period of calm and peace. It certainly is different from those reactive emotional outbursts where the amygdala in the brain overrides everything else and takes control. These episodes usually involve too much force, panic, and even desperation in your views. In fact, learning the difference between making calm intuitive decisions and emotional ones evidences a brilliant self- awareness; and if you can improve this, it's one of the most effective bits of intelligence you can ever gain.

Qualifications and courses

In the brilliant movie 'The Wizard of Oz', the Wizard says to the scarecrow:

"Back where I come from we have universities, seats of great learning—where men go to become great thinkers. And when they come out, they think deep thoughts—and with no more brains than you have. But! They have one thing you haven't got! A diploma!"[61]

A fantastic way to boost knowledge is to take a course or begin studying for a qualification. You can take courses in almost any topic now with so much expertise growing. Areas that are relevant to our topic here are sports psychology, fitness and health, nutrition, sports coaching, neuro-linguistic programming, parenting, leadership, life coaching, learning science, cognitive behavioral therapy etc.

One of the benefits of attending courses is that you meet other people who usually have similar experiences to yours and are in a mindset to learn and debate. The courses that I have attended and taught have been brilliant for this social aspect and have been as important to the learning as the actual information being delivered in the course. It helps because these people are strangers to begin with and therefore you feel more honest and confident to share your stories with them. Guided by the teachers, the sharing of stories and problems between the participants brings a richness to the course structure. In my experience, people normally make some good friends too.

Lately there has been a rise in online webinars and distance learning which has made qualifications much more accessible at a whole range of levels. You may not get the social interaction benefits discussed above, but you do get to study at home and costs can be much cheaper.

The beauty of taking qualifications these days is that the flexibility, depth, and range are boundless. You can complete a PhD course that takes many years or a 2 hour workshop that gives a certificate of completion. Find the course that suits you and go for it. And for some, like the Scarecrow in the Wizard of Oz, a confirmation written down on paper is all they need to believe in themselves more and let out the wisdom they had all along!

Practical experiences

I guess this is the one that most sports parents are going through naturally week by week, year by year. Never underestimate the chance to learn something new each time you go with your child to sport.

The value of trial and error is arguably your greatest source of education. I often wonder what generations of people did before teaching and learning arrived on earth! How did they survive and progress? My guess is that they found what worked well and eliminated what did not. Well, at least those that grew and survived. I urge you to try out different things with your children and find out what works well and what does not. I know this must sound patronizing because you have already done this so much with your children. I am just encouraging you to do it a little more formally. Come up with ideas and simply test them out and keep notes.

A very easy and helpful method is keeping a diary based on the following questions:

1. *What did I learn today about the way I went about trying to help my kids?*
2. *What could I do next time to help more?*

Over the course of a few months you will start to compile a list of learnings that through trial and error you have found to work well and not so well.

This is something I started two years ago when going to tournaments with my wife. It has helped me tremendously. I make a quick read through my own lessons before she plays, and it settles me down into a place where I become helpful, not a hindrance.

Here are some of my notes to myself:

- Stay chilled, laugh beforehand, ring friend or do exercise.
- Sit next to a friend who has a calming effect.
- TRUST Laura, she is doing this for her and will find a way.
- Keep your hands still and just smile when she looks at you.
- If she needs inspiration, show your fist.
- Don't drink coffee beforehand (too pumped).

- If you are feeling critical, go and sit on your own and watch. DO NOT CRITICIZE HER TO OTHERS.

It is amazing how many times I forget simple things I have learned. Without the diary on my phone; I would be struggling much more.

Too Much? - Beware of paralysis by analysis!

One of the downsides of seeking lots of knowledge is that you can become addicted to it and then get swamped by it. I also believe you fall into a belief trap that all the right answers exist somewhere. Often there are no right answers, just signposts. I always tell my players that I am at best a 'map maker' for them. I point to certain truths, warn of potential dangers, and provide some clues for their pursuit of what they are looking for. I believe this is a good metaphor for how we could view all education experiences. Having the wisdom to know that only signposts exist and that the real truth is in your personal context is liberating. It frees you from the burden of not knowing enough. I have witnessed many people eagerly pursue knowledge in a bid to overcome their fear of inadequacy. I have even seen colleagues at the university panic about this too as they aim to produce research paper after research paper. Out of genuine passion, some do it well and are aware of the limitations; but those that go deeper and deeper searching for the 'one truth' to a problem can end up out of touch with normal life. Their quest and thirst for knowledge stifles them, and as they stack it up too high they form a barrier so dense that they lose sight of the person stood right in front of them.

Summary

Educate yourself in the best way for you. Take in the appropriate **amount** of fuel for you and your engine. Try some new methods in acquiring knowledge that you may not have trusted before, e.g. taking a class in psychology. Informal learning and formal learning are as valuable and credible as each other.

Information from inside of you is just as good as information coming in from outside of you. Keep a diary of what works well and what does not.

You can forget simple things. Don't get swamped by the pressure to know more. You will never know enough if you feel this way. Wisdom is the application of education in your life, with your children.

Notes & Reminders

Flight Path: Stage 4

'Lead Through Example'

Stage 4: Take Off 'Lead through Example'

No written word nor spoken plea can teach our youth what they should be. Nor all the books on all the shelves. It's what the teachers are themselves.[62]

Anonymous poem used by John Wooden

So now it is time to take off. Taking off is perhaps the most uncomfortable stage for some because it involves a shock to the system and a change in altitude. For others it is the most exciting part. Here we are in the area of your actual behaviors as opposed to your thoughts, which we covered in stages 1 and 2. This is the stage where it is what you do and don't do that counts the most. As Mahatma Gandhi viewed leadership: *"Be the change you want to see".*[63]

"My Father has always been my hero and I have always admired him. While he's never been an emotional man or one who shows a lot of his feelings, he always could bring some calm to a situation, and say the right thing at the right time to me. I wanted to be just like him. As an adult I see a lot of him in myself. And a lot of those characteristics helped me to achieve the success I did."[64]

Michael Johnson, Four-time Olympic Gold and eight-time World Champion

You may be aware as you get older just how much your own parents and grandparents influenced your life values. You may have wandered off in all different directions and different lines of work, and held contrasting beliefs about things; but when it comes down to what is really important in life, at least one of your parents very much set the scene. For some this can be things like work ethic or community values; for others it may be humility or self-respect. It is something that is more appreciated as people move past the striving years into middle age and of course have their own teenagers to deal with. Suddenly one day you think: "Wow, am I turning into my mother?"

"My Dad, who was a farmer, taught me the ethos of working hard. You'd see him go out at 5.30 in the morning and come back in late. Now looking back at that dedication, he loved what he did – and that focus and hard work was instilled in me from early on."[65]

Sally Gunnell, World and Olympic Champion

Damned if you do, damned if you don't!

Copying our parents is not always a deliberate thing, far from it in fact. Often, youngsters, especially teenagers, strive to be individual and independent of parents. The years where teens famously start grunting responses or telling their parents how wrong and out of touch they are is a common case. There is almost a rebellion by teenagers to any of their parent's ideas and opinions as they strive to prove how much they don't need them! Suddenly a parent's support is now intrusion, their simple questions now an inquisition, and their public affection is now embarrassing. In sport, the same comments that once motivated now demotivate. Where you eased pressure you are now the cause of it and your organizational expertise is now over fussing. You can end up in a no-win situation, a 'dammed if you do and dammed if you don't' scenario where you feel stuck and frustrated.

Reflection:

Have you had this experience? Is it happening to you now?

Your Intentions		Received as
Provide support	=	Intrusion
Ask a simple question	=	Inquisition
Show affection	=	Embarrassing
To help organize	=	Fussing
Help Motivate	=	Pressure
Try to relax them	=	Molly-Coddling

What usually happens in these cases?

Such episodes are just reminders of how difficult it is to avoid frustrations and conflicts in the life of a sports parent. The best case here is a reduction of the frequency and the intensity of the clashes, certainly not a complete removal of them. Just by noticing that the approach you currently use seems to get no improvements, apart from making you feel better as you get things off your chest, I believe you will start to try different methods of helping your children along. You have most probably been the one misreading positive intent at some point in your life, likely even with your own parents. Just know it is part of life, accept it more, and adapt it accordingly.

Your example lasts longer than your words?

While your words may be misinterpreted and shut out, your actions are not as easily ignored.

> *"Whatever good values and standards of ethics that I have today, I attribute to my association with John Wooden, and looking at his values and learning from him, the standards he set, the character he acted out. What he not only spoke about, but acted and lived, has held me in very good stead."[66]*

Stan Jacobs on John Wooden

John Wooden, one of the most revered coaches in the history of sports, believed deeply in his own parent's values and life lessons. It was watching his father work hard day in day out that he credited his lead by example approach.

> *"Don't be a character, have character. A parent can help direct a child when it comes to goals. Show leadership. Show discipline. Show industriousness. Have traditional values. The person you are is the person your child will become."[67]*

John Wooden

Contradictions weaken your message

> *"Video meliora proboque deteriora sequor."[68]*

> *"I see and approve of the better, but I follow the worse."*

Metamorphoses VII. 20–21 of Ovid.

Not many people will react well to the messages of those who preach, but fail to follow their own advice. Youngsters do not need to know the meaning of the word hypocrite to sense a person who doesn't 'walk the walk'. These people simply lack congruence and conviction. "Talk is cheap" as they say! Do you recognize any of these below?

- *The overweight personal trainer telling you how easy it is lose weight.*
- *The nervous parent telling you not to be nervous.*

- *The complainer complaining about those who complain!*
- *The smoker telling you to be healthy.*
- *The boxer telling his daughter not to become a fighter.*
- *The womanizer telling his son to treat women with respect.*
- *The unpunctual coach telling you to be on time.*
- *The drug abusing athlete campaigning about fairness and transparency.*
- *Aggressive parents telling their children that calmness is the way.*
- *The passive father telling his daughter to stand up to competitors.*
- *The quitter asking you to give more when you perform.*

Perhaps you have your own examples of the hypocrite to offer. What I ask you to consider is this: **Have you ever been inspired by somebody who failed to back up what they preach in the way they are as a person?**

You can't help the poor by being one of them!

This claim, like many, is attributed to Abraham Lincoln. I always wonder how Presidents and Prime Ministers cope. With so many decisions and worldly concerns, how do they find the mental space to deal with personal day-to-day things as the rest of us do? It seems they do find a way to cope, and nobody could question Lincoln's ability to deal well with both aspects of his life.

The gist of Lincoln's wisdom here is that first and foremost you have to be strong yourself to help others, particularly those weaker. There is no value in beating yourself into the ground in a bid to help everyone. It is from a position of personal strength and clarity that one can help others. In similar ways good support for your children comes from emotional security, from self-appreciation, and doing your best job. Not many parents who themselves lack confidence, emotional security, and conviction do well with this issue. The most supportive and useful parents appear to be the ones who are comfortable within. They live fulfilled lives and do not seek extra from their child's journey. They are of course involved with the child and can spend many hours with them, but they do not seek to steal too much emotionally from the child. They are given it freely by the child as they develop into the child's rock of support.

Neuroscientist Linda Rock backs this up in her excellent book, <u>Coaching with the Brain in Mind</u>:

"When we feel safe, we humans are explorers, approaching new discoveries with delight. If people are anxious, uncomfortable, or fearful, they do not learn. That is, they do not build new brain connections or create new ideas. Knowing how to create the conditions for learning is a key skill for coaches/parents."[69]

So young competitors are best surrounded by confident, calm, and self-assured leaders. Their brains will go to a place where they can experiment, take risks, and generate new ideas. By knowing they are accepted for themselves and by knowing that calm people will not antagonize them for demonstrating imagination and creativity, they march on with confidence and reassurance. Feeling secured and supported by you rather than panicked and overwhelmed, you will act like their own personal beaming lighthouse, there for them even when the storms are strong.

Although a simple concept, this is by no means easy. We all have our own fears and stresses yet we also have many, many qualities. Focus on these qualities you have because they will settle you. You don't really lack anything you need. The feeling of 'lack' is a destroyer of many things. It dents your confidence and results in paranoia. It stiffens your inventiveness and makes you vulnerable. It takes away faith to just be you.

So go forward trying your best to be strong and fulfilled in yourself. Keep a zest for your own personal dreams, hobbies, and ambitions. With you feeling excited, proud of yourself and alive, you will show the way to those you love by who you are and how you choose to live this one life you have.

A pound of inspiration is worth a ton of motivation

Inspiration is that wonderful powerful force that simply puts you in a positive mission state. When you are inspired you will find yourself doing the things that need to be done to reach your goal. You really do not need motivation when you are inspired because in your mind you are already completely committed to the task at hand. Enthusiasm is high and energy seems to never end. It's like a force has gotten inside you and it lifts your mood, your outlook, and self-belief. You can almost feel this inspiration in your heart and stomach. When you are inspired you complain less, doubt less, and feel less tired. You have an end goal in mind, but you enjoy the jobs at hand just as much. You feel proud, often humble and connected to something more purposeful than just yourself.

Motivation is also a very powerful force. Words like 'willpower' and 'grind' are highly necessary commodities if you want to succeed in life and sport at competitive levels. There are times when you just need to find a reason to work. It may be the thought of a reward that gets you going or it may be avoiding failure that drives you on. Using threats and punishments as well as rewards and bribes certainly get people going. Another form of powerful motivation is personal vanity. How much energy will we spend trying to look good? Trying to fit in and be accepted for the image we want to portray is highly motivational. Not many of us forget to wear the clothes we choose to when we go to a party or ceremony. You will no doubt be aware of how urgent your teenagers suddenly need the latest trend of clothes, phone, or sports gear. They must avoid being embarrassed by their peers at all costs and hopefully be admired for their excellent ability to keep up with the latest agreed fashions.

Before you mock youngsters for this, adults are just as motivated to keep a favorable image with their peers. The amount of conversations I have overheard where sports parents cleverly battle each other to justify small failures and brag about small successes is staggering. Being completely honest here, I do it myself! I have heard that the ideal salary is $8,000 more than your brother or sister in law!

The need to maintain popularity, to be a success, to be liked, to be loved, to do everything correctly, and avoid making life a mess drives on a lot of us. It may not be the healthiest, and it can be exhausting, but we cannot deny its force. So the need to avoid perceived failings and the desire for rewards is in basic terms how motivation works: Powerful and stressful.

The difference between motivation and inspiration is subtle, but the differences in how they affect you are HUGE

- *Where motivation is demanding, inspiration is giving.*
- *Where motivation can be harsh, inspiration is gentle.*
- *Where motivation fades and needs topping up, inspiration endures.*
- *Where motivation targets the brain, inspiration fills the whole body.*
- *Where motivation can cost a lot of money and time, inspiration is free and quick.*
- *Where motivation needs to convince you, inspiration has you already convinced.*
- *Where motivation presumes effort, inspiration feels effortless.*
- *Where motivation is a means to an end, inspiration is joyful in itself.*

- *Where motivation focuses on future goals, inspiration is present and now.*

Compare the difference between those times where:

A) *You have to remind your children to complete a task and then explain the reasons why. Example: Go to training tonight; it will make you faster.*

B) *Those situations where they are just bursting to do a task because they just want to do it. Example: Dad, can I do five minutes more training please. I'm loving playing!*

'**A**' requires motivation techniques, '**B**' does not!

Of course it is hard to expect that your children will be in a permanent state of scenario 'B' (inspiration), but it is better the more they are in this position. I have witnessed many youngsters when they are in the 'sampling' phases of sports having lots of fun, play, and inspiration. As they get older and more proficient in a sport, for whatever personal reasons many youngsters start to spend more time requiring motivation, and this can be most common when they reach the 'investment' years. This in turn puts more pressure on parents who see a drop off in inspiration, natural fun, and love of the sport, and consequently they find themselves having to use more and more motivation methods to get their children to play.

This then causes a shift in power, as the youngster starts to play for other reasons than fun and love. The parents who resist this trap and do not panic by trying to be their child's motivation do best in the long-term. There may be gentle reminders and even encouragement to continue, but 'Winning Parents' recognize when the candle of inspiration has gone out. Then instead of trying to force it, they relax, give some room, go about their own lives positively, and wait until inspiration strikes again. The 'Winning Parent' has the ability to understand that without love, passion, and inspiration for a sport, their child will go only towards dejection and eventually despair.

BURNOUT: Constant motivation without inspiration.

In my experience of working with young athletes the one thing above all else I notice causing problems is when the fun disappears **for too long**. Whenever I see a child playing a sport looking as if they are miserable, I know what comes next: Stress! Somehow what was previously an enjoyable activity becomes a source of strain as the young athlete begins to look for other rewards and benefits from it. I have pondered on this very much, and I have wondered what goes wrong.

You never hear about a depressed dolphin or a bird who can't be bothered to fly? You will rarely see a dog that refrains from jumping up and down wagging its tail with glee the moment you let it know it's going for a walk! The reason is that they simply derive joy and pleasure from the activity itself. They simply just want to swim, fly, or run.

Children are like joyful animals when they find an activity that they like. If I ever leave sports equipment lying around where there are children you can bet your house they will just pick it up and play with it for fun. I used to tell them to leave the equipment alone until I realized how much I was having a battle with nature, which one rarely wins! Is there anything more wonderful than seeing young children focused and immersed in fun, laughing, trying, and fighting to improve? It is such a natural and healthy state it can really be very warming to watch. Free of consequences, free of what it all means, and free of worry, what a joy it is to see a child with inspiration coursing through them.

Take a moment to reflect upon these scenarios:

- *Do you have a particular memory of this with your own child? A time where they were free? Try and just recall it and enjoy it for a few moments...*

- *How have things been lately when they play a sport? Has it changed over the years?*

- *How have you tried so far to help them get back to their natural childlike and inspired state? Have you had any success?*

- *Is there any way you may have contributed to making their sports experiences more of a 'means to an end' environment, a thing they do to prove things about themselves and your family tribe?*

As I have mentioned, there is nothing wrong with motivation and real life lessons that competitive sport can pressure you with. The danger is when the inspiration has gone. That is when you are 'beating a dead horse'. You can unknowingly cause major damage in these times and possibly create a fear of sports competition as things go further and further downhill. Unfortunately, I have witnessed this happen all too often and the saddest part is that the parents are always just trying to help. Everyone has been temporarily deluded into believing that the important thing is winning at all costs. Of course winning is important – that is the essence of competition. However, even the most fundamental winners surely accept that emotional health, socialization, and physical wellbeing are top of the list when it comes to children.

Amazingly, some children can handle it and get stronger from it, but these are rare and even then the long-term effects of forced effort can take its toll. For most children it is too much too early. Too much praise, too much criticism. Too much adulation, too much embarrassment. Too much attention, too much rejection. Too many expectations, too many disappointments. Too much!!!

Just as how timing is the essence of comedy, knowing your child's personal limits are essential to quality nurturing. The very best race horse trainers are experts in this area. They know what happens when a horse loses its enthusiasm to race. They know how much to push and when to just retire them to a field for a long rest. I believe 'Winning Parents' follow this premise with their children.

Inspiration is personal

Who knows why we feel inspired by different things? Nature, people, stories, animals, films, accomplishments, art, music, the list goes on. It is difficult to always articulate why we exactly feel inspired by something; yet the one thing that is common in all cases is that we have been affected deeply. Courage and bravery can be sources; acts of great forgiveness or kindness affect many. For me, achievement after great perseverance and overcoming struggle get to me every time. Dignity under duress is powerful; beauty and awe can be another source. Love is often involved at the same level, and of course a person's vision of God can be the ultimate inspiration.

Golfing superstar Jordan Spieth, who has been lauded by many for his noticeable level of maturity and likeability is clearly inspired by his sister Ellie. He claims:

"I love having her around. She's an incredible sister, my biggest supporter. She is somebody who you can watch and then reflect on the big picture of life and understand that all these frustrations in a day, or in a round of golf, are really secondary.

Ellie certainly is the best thing that's happened in our family. It helps put things in perspective. I'm lucky to play on tour and to compete with these guys, it has been a dream come true. I definitely attribute a lot of that to her.

She's the funniest person in our family. It's humbling to see her and her friends and the struggles they go through each day that we take for granted, where it seems easy for us and it's not for them. At the same time, they are the happiest people in the world. And when I say 'they,' I speak to special needs kids. My experience with her and with her friends, it's fantastic. I love being part of it, helping support it."[70]

Take a moment to think about inspiration: Who has inspired you in your life? What inspires you today? Do you have a movie or specific scene from one that affects you? A piece of music? Just notice that inspired feeling now and feel that energy rush through your body. Great isn't it? Do you believe you inspire other people? Do you have an inspirational effect on your children, or do you find you are more of a motivator?

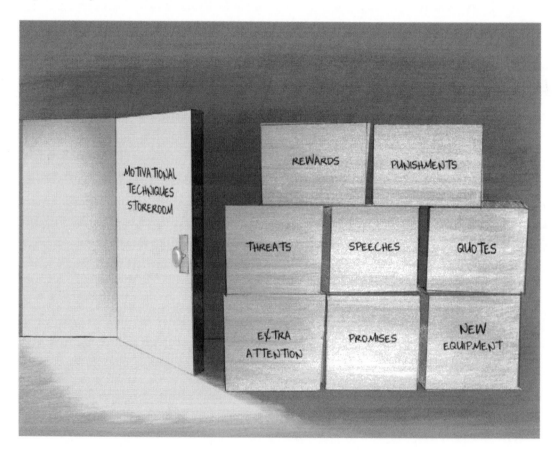

'A pound of inspiration is as powerful as a ton of motivation'

Children want your inspiration not only your motivation!

In my experience most young people want to be inspired by their family and especially their parents, though they may find it hard to admit. The strong ones want to react positively to your lead and join you in your world of strength. The weaker ones may rebel at first, possibly being overwhelmed by your high standards but in time as they mature and live life, they will benefit from your leadership in action. Remember this, your children will naturally:

- *Want to look up to you.*
- *Want to be proud of you.*
- *Want to tell their friends about how great you are and what you do.*
- *Want to see strength, conviction, and control under pressure.*
- *Want to know that you are steady and someone they can come to for advice.*

Of course, you will still need to inject motivation techniques because times can be tough, life is real. Giving the occasional reality check is vital even with the most level headed of youngsters. Competitive sport itself is brilliant at giving reality checks, and it can do a lot of the motivation for you. *I have found that the best parents are the ones who leave motivation to the pain of defeat or the joy of winning and improvement.* They resist adding extra consequences, apportioning blame, or expressing anger. Naturally, there are the happy and normal celebrations associated with pride of victory and the pangs of disappointment associated with loss, but these are often in scale and in balance with the reality that they are dealing with youth sport. The best parents keep this perspective, and that really helps everyone concerned. I am always inspired myself by people who can show such dignity and calm in such pressing family circumstances.

Time for a Cup of T! (Parenting under pressure)

It would be fair to assume that sports performers will have to deal with performing under pressure at some stage of their development. We all consider pressure differently and react accordingly. Whatever it is that causes pressure, it remains imperative that the performer has the skills to cope and respond in a positive way. So central to the coaching and parental process must be the ability in helping athletes with such skills. In his excellent book, Think Like a Winner, Yehuda Shinar proposes 12 key qualities of being able to perform under pressure. He calls this 'T-CUP' (*Thinking correctly under pressure*).[71]

The 12 consistent behaviors he has compiled and witnessed in people who can 'Think correctly under pressure' are as follows:

- *Create their own opportunities.*
- *Seize those opportunities.*
- *Maintain the momentum.*
- *Strive for the best possible result.*
- *Avoid unnecessary corners – don't repeat mistakes they will make!*
- *Stick to what they know works for them.*
- *Give up what does not work.*
- *Get back to basics when required.*
- *Improve self-control.*
- *Make correct decisions.*
- *Learn to thrive under pressure.*
- *Maximize the use of time.*

BE CAREFUL

Exhibit your own emotional control!

The English writer Dorothy Nevill once proclaimed:

"The real art of conversation is not only to say the right thing at the right place but to leave unsaid the wrong thing at the tempting moment".[72]

It is so tempting to lose your cool after watching your children compete. For hours, the emotions can reign on. Be mindful of this because this is where you can do some serious damage. During these moments, the 'Winning Parent' is able to reflect on and appreciate what is happening; and they are capable of transmitting restraint and composure. What is said (or not said) at this time is absolutely imperative, as your children think this is the truth. They see the 'mask off', and in their world it is your true feelings. Even an apology won't erase their belief although at least they will forgive you.

All of the T-CUP behaviors require independence and good levels of self-awareness. People who know what they want, how to get it, and what they will have when they get it are well on the road to independence. Most important of all **they do it**, and they can do this when under all the various forms of pressure that sport and life throws up.

I challenge you as parents to work on 3 of the TCUP behaviors proposed.

My 3 TCUP areas to get better at:

My ideas for helping me improve at them are:

Leading by example is arguably the most powerful form of leadership as it gains instant respect. Youngsters whether they know it or not will constantly be thinking, "If they can't do it for themselves, how can they preach to me with confidence?" So it is important that your effort levels in areas you feel are important are up there. People will want to see the same sort of qualities in you that you are asking of them. Not necessarily at their level but at your own best level. If you are asking your young competitors to push themselves harder in an agreed area of improvement it doesn't half improve the power of your message if you yourself are or aren't pushing hard in an area of your own life.

Here are some ideas:

- **Undertake a new personal challenge and see it through**. It could be in any endeavor. Go through training and practice, strive to improve.

- **Perform under pressure**. Sing a song, or deliver a speech in public – this will remind you of your coping skills.

- **When you fail at something, recognize it, accept it, recover from it, fail again etc**. Hold it together, lose with dignity, if that's what you want to see in the children.

- **When you next achieve something act with dignity**. Be proud of yourself, and **do not** use it to exemplify their inferiority.

- **Join them in a challenge**. Want them to lose weight? Do it yourself! Want them to develop fitness? Get fit yourself!

- **Work together on a project away from sport**. Show them the qualities you have, e.g. gardening, building a shed, looking after an animal/pet.

Summary

*Your kids will copy **who you are** far more than what you say. Provide more inspiration, less motivation.*

Avoid burnout. Notice when the inspiration has gone, and it's just too much 'a means to an end'.

Avoid coming across as a hypocrite. Working on yourself will improve your children in the long-term as they see your example.

T-CUP: Learning to Think correctly under pressure will make you a lighthouse of calm even in through the strong storms.

Notes & Reminders

Flight Path: Stage 5

'Patience, Empathy, and Humility'

Stage 5: Be a Co-Pilot 'Patience, Empathy, and Humility'

This is the stage where you try your best to take a back seat, sit back, and let the journey unfold. You **are not** in charge of this particular flight, your son or daughter is. They are the captains while you switch between the roles of co-pilot and passenger. Like all good co-pilots you are highly skilled, supportive, calming, and you exude confidence in yourself and the pilot. You are there for serious emergencies but other than that you are there to assist when requested.

- *The pilot may have their own ways of doing things but you have **patience** for that.*

- *You have deep understanding what it feels like to have the responsibility and pressure of captain, so you have **empathy.***

- *You are happy not to take any credit for the journey although your role has been vital, so you have shown **humility** and developed it in your child too.*

Patience: Are you about the long-term or now?

Patience is the quality that will enable you to achieve the most effective results, not merely the most immediate results. In my work with coaching graduates I teach a lecture called *'coaching for the long-term versus coaching for **now**.'* In essence, when working in professional sports situations the **now** is quite important. Funding and livelihoods at stake, there is more urgency to achieve short-term results, and therefore this affects the pressure of the coaching process and the coaching strategy. If you want to understand this more, just put on your sports news channel right now and see how long it takes for a report to come on about somebody who is going to be sacked or who is in an unrecoverable slump. Then wait for the so called 'expert' pundit (normally an ex-professional player) joining in with the drama and fueling the pressure of this urgent results catastrophe. Fans will no doubt be shown with depressed faces and even tears in some instances. They voice their panic and anger at the injustice of the whole thing and complain of the incompetence of anyone who can be apportioned with blame. Patience has long since departed. We want results **now**!

With youth players, who are in need of experience, growth in their body, and development of mind, it is the medium to long-term future that is emphasized. This gives coaches more time to play with and in turn should reduce tension and pressure over results. Here the emphasis is on patience and experimentation as sport remains a playground for development. Results are valued to some degree, and certain levels of pressure can harden some characters (though break many others); yet an emphasis on effort and performance targets are equally if not more so important.

This is a situation where learning and enjoyment is top priority because it is basically not urgent or affecting their livelihood. The coach and player have time to play with, and consequently patience should be abundant and central to the philosophy of all involved.

"My parents have never really been ones to intervene. They are the antithesis of the pushy parents so prevalent around sport and schools. My coach and I would go to English schools competitions and be amazed at the pressure heaped on the kids by their parents. It was sad to see and it made you understand why so many dropped out of sport. In fairness to my coach 'Chell', he always had a long-term plan. Many coaches want the reflected glory of their athletes' trophies and titles, but Chell was never like that. He was in it for the long haul and said the plan was not to make me a great youth performer but a great future athlete. For someone with an impatient streak, that was hard to grasp, but I am glad that I did not have a coach or parents living out their dreams through me and driving me headlong towards burnout."[73]

Jessica Ennis, Olympic and World Champion

Natural Play

If you watch children go and set up their own game of something they generally manage. They adapt rules, define how to succeed, officiate themselves, and compete. They learn skills, get fit, learn how to win, and learn how to lose. They go about participating in their natural way and then they participate accordingly. Most of us did lots of our learning like this. We were urgent to win that little contest and we could have some fierce battles and sometimes a few fights, but never once did we feel the pressure of our coaches or families bearing down on us. **"Did you win?"** was never a question asked. Your parents were simply glad to have you back safe and well exercised, even if a little dirty! In the absence of adults, we were patient with ourselves.

In a nutshell, developmental coaching has the luxury of time and all youth coaching should be thought of as developmental, thus allowing patience to flourish.

Professionals do not always have the luxury of time, so pressure exists to win now, thus reducing patience below those levels afforded to youth athletes.

As a parent, what do you think about this? Have you found this clear cut? Do you find that your patience comes easily with your child's sports development?

Professional Junior?

Is there such a term? Can you have a professional child sports performer? Is it even legal? Would they pay tax? Have you ever seen one?

What about the term ***Professional Junior Parent?*** A parent who believes they have a child who is professional? I am sure I have seen some! Do you know any?

All tongue in cheek here of course, but maybe it got you thinking a bit. I do believe some parents forget that they are dealing with children not professional players. I call it 'Professional Junior Syndrome".

> ***Professional Junior Syndrome:*** *The tendency to treat a child sports performer as if they are someone who earns their living from the sport they play.*

This is one of the major blocks to patience. It is a big misread of the situation your child is in. It can creep up on you very unexpectedly, particularly after small successes and local media attention.

Tendencies

- *An over-emphasis on results causing panic and worry.*

- *A loss of patience with your child and occasionally their coaches or teammates.*

- *Your personal mood is dependent upon results (the reverse dependency trap).*

- *A necessity to own the best equipment and sports kit available.*

- *An urgency to talk about your child's accomplishments when meeting new people.*

- *A pre-occupation to rescue and fix all their performance problems right away.*

- *Using social media to build up the profile and image of your child.*

- *Fortune telling in regards to why or why not they will make it as a professional.*

- *Dominant topic of conversation with friends and family; particularly noticeable away from the performance environment.*

- *Continuously over-analyzing your child's performance level.*

- *Constantly comparing your child to other players/teammates to ascertain where they stand in the 'pecking order' (something frequently witnessed in team sports).*

Antidote: Remember the REALITY!

The reality is that children are young performers learning a sport which they may play professionally one day. At which time, they will be good enough and mature enough to make their own decisions, with support from those they have come to trust. If they still trust you when they get to this stage and feel that they can take on your advice, you will have most probably been on a winning path. Somewhere along the line, they kept faith in you. You managed not to frighten them off or control them to the point of despair. Some part of your nurturing skills was wise enough not to push too hard or blame too much when things went wrong for a while. You had intuition not to get wrapped up in early celebrations of success or add to the hype that coaches and other children begin to build when they do well. Maybe you had the quality of great **patience**.

The big picture: Be urgent but do not panic

Things move on quickly in sport, and yes, it is important that measureable progress is made in relation to competition. It is a fine art knowing when to push harder or when to have a break. What will not help here is panicking. What will help is patient reflection and then decisive action. This is where it will be crucial to step back and do whatever helps you think about the bigger picture. Go back to your definition of winning (Stage 2) and check on those agreed values you discussed. Use the medium of time to help you see a different perspective.

You could use the past: When my child was born how important was it to me that they succeeded at sport compared to how they would simply be happy in life with whatever they chose to do?

Or you could use the future: In a year from now, will this thing causing us stress today be important? Will we even remember it?

Or can you think about the end of days: When I look back on all my life, what will I wish had done more of and how important will this issue seem to me then?

I personally use the last example the most. In fact, I probably utilize that scenario most days. At first it feels a bit morbid, but I have found it to be incredibly uplifting as I begin to appreciate each day more fully. It really helps me when I am watching my wife compete or when results don't go the way we want them to. I could have done with implementing this last point more when I was a bit younger!

It is incredibly helpful to know and accept that success often requires many ups and downs. Understanding that drops in the standard of performance and fluctuations in motivation are just part of the path. It helps you maintain patience in times when you and your child need it the most. It also helps you to keep your feet on the ground after those sudden bursts of improvement and occasional successes when it is tempting to go too high. This following picture of success is always helpful:

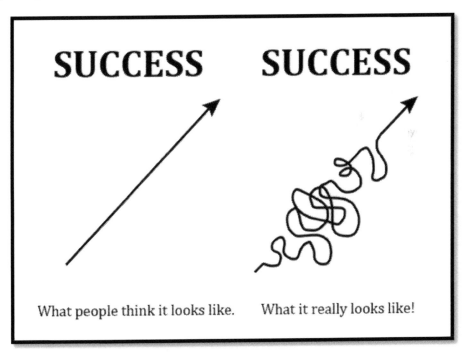

You will show your children a lot of your character when they win. You will reveal all of it when they lose.

Keep patience from being a lost art

We live in a fast-paced world of instant coffee, instant microwave meals, fast food restaurants, lightning speed computers, and even faster wireless internet. Many things in life are easier to acquire compared with how things were in previous generations. Some things certainly make our daily routines considerably more efficient, productive, and stress-free. I think we can all testify to this fact. But success is often judged by what we own, our status within society, and how we compare with our peers. In particular, **patience** is becoming a lost art. We are consistently bombarded with tales of success; we want some of it, and so do our children. We want it right now! If we don't get it, we can tend to panic and seek out 'quick-fix' solutions that will elevate our concern.

Adam Henley:

"The one thing I see is too much pressure being put on youngsters very early. I've seen so many talented players come and go. I was never a 'top tier' player growing up all the way through the age groups; so I think it helped keep my feet on the ground. My expectations were lower than all these 'top young stars' that were talked about. You could see parents had a bit of swagger about them and when it started to go wrong as they got older; they couldn't handle it so well. So they got negative and caused pressure. It was like a fall from grace.

I think the parents wanted it too much, maybe more than the player sometimes. They were kind of too desperate for the 'dream'. They perhaps got over-involved and felt like it was them 'making it' or not. I don't know really, just a sense you get. It's such a very long journey in Academy soccer, from aged 7 to 18 there are so many variables. You can't have pressure and expectation all that time. It's got to be fun and enjoyable but some parents just couldn't get that. They were too intense analyzing things and demanding improvements".

Scott Fitzgerald:

"I always went to my dad for advice really. He has been like an advisor more than anything. He was always very relaxed with me and my decisions around boxing; he never put pressure on me even though you could tell he wanted me to do really well. You don't want your son losing at boxing because you can get hurt, but he never got too heavy on me.

Dad spent lots of his time with me. He trained me and took me all over the place visiting professional gyms. At one point we would be going to Bolton (40 miles round trip) almost every day. I think he managed to get me to 'dream big' without making me feel the pressure of it. He gave me small goals to achieve and said I could definitely get to be a National Champion one day which I didn't believe at the time. He managed to put confidence into me and timed everything just right. He was patient with me yet trained me hard when I needed to get the work in. He never pushed me though. I think because he used to box, he knows what it is like so he has good experience."

Lauren Quigley:

"Sometimes I've seen parents telling their kids off on poolside when they've been beaten in a race. This is especially true when expectations are high because there has been too much hype about the swimmer who has lost. In swimming, standards change quickly and just because you were quick one year doesn't mean you will be the next, especially at the youth level. So some families who think they've got a little superstar can't handle it when they don't win like they did before. It is like they panic. They don't see the long journey.

Don't get me wrong, my mother told me off a few times but never on poolside in front of everyone and never about winning or losing. It was when I couldn't be bothered and didn't apply myself. I think it was fair to tell me off for this, I needed that sometimes.

Lots of those swimmers who were the next big thing quit when they got older. I think lots of that was because of pressure and disappointment from parents and some coaches when they had tough days."

The 'Winning Parent' is the one who can ***keep the art of patience alive*** in this pressurized world of urgency and instant celebrity. That is celebrity within your family, the communities you are part of, and then the wider public. Social media sites such as Facebook, Instagram, and Twitter have illuminated the potential for small successes to be promoted in your respective communities instantly and repeatedly. This is a 'tender trap' you may need to watch out for. Pride is one thing, but, "look at how amazing my child is everyone," is a completely different thing! Believe me when I say that I have seen the consequences of over-hyping children after small successes. Pressure builds and expectations rise to unrealistic proportions; it simply becomes too much for many youngsters to deal with. Soon those children have nowhere to go but down from the pedestal their peers and parents have subtly and not so subtly placed them on.

Your children might not appreciate the effort and emotional control that it takes for you to display such strength in those tempting and trying times, but they sure will as they get older and look back at the way you treated them. Your rewards will come down the line because your children will never have a phobia response to sport. They will not have anchored feelings of shame, guilt, or disappointment when they think about sport, and so they will come back to it all their lives with vigor, passion, and positive intent. Keep your faith in the long process, remember your love for your children for who they are, not for what they achieve on the sports field.

Let the sport be the teacher

If you have the patience to let it, the best coach of all can be the sport itself. Its challenges and emotional tests will present themselves to the performers as they strive to improve. Opponents, rules, fitness demands, teamwork requirements, performance conditions, injuries etc. will all force youngsters to adapt and rethink their approaches. This is a natural part of the fun and appeal of sport; encountering varied challenges and attempting to deal with them with a determined and robust outlook. Mastery is never attained although it is searched for, and therefore learning to show patience is a wonderful gift that sport teaches your child.

We have seen people, without the virtue of patience turn to cheating, with drug use being prevalent in some sports. These cheats have failed to meet the challenge they encountered. They have run out of patience and been unable to cope with the challenge they had been set. So they cheated and made up their own rules; they have taken the easy way out at that precise moment.

We do not want our youth running out of patience with challenges. We do not want them to take short cuts and make up their own sports by changing the rules for themselves. What we really want to see in our youth is an ability to overcome challenges put before them, and sport is such a normal and healthy way to do this. It is your duty as parents to be **patient** too. Today when challenges are momentarily too hard and the sport and all its competitors too tough, you need to be the bedrock of acceptance and patience. You have to align yourself with the principles of life itself. Just as an organic gardener and caring farmer works with nature's pace, you too must resist the temptations of the forced and unnatural approach.

As Basma El Shorbagy said in her revealing interview in Stage 2 'Define Winning':

"I learned a lot from Mohamed's first coach. He set a great mentality in us all. He said, "If you lose, you go back to work and work harder than before". This has been very important and helps after some of the lows times."

Recently a parent of a player I coach said a wise thing to me about the nature of sport and how it had helped build character in his son. He said:

"It took my son a long time to realize that a sport is not like schoolwork. At school he works hard and gets the rewards almost right away. What he puts in, he gets back. In sport, he doesn't always get that. He puts in hours of work and doesn't always get the rewards, and it frustrates him. He'd say to me, "Why am I doing all this work and practice and I am still losing to the same players?" I would remind him that his opponents are working hard too and he is chasing moving targets. He has come to accept this more and been a lot more patient with himself. I love this because to me that is real character and that is what life is like after school."

I thought this was a brilliant summary, and it was wonderful to hear a parent being so steady and patient with their son's sports journey. It makes sense why his son is not only a brilliant improver (and getting better results steadily) but also a well-rounded young man.

Variations in maturation rates

Another reason that patience with youngsters must be demonstrated is due to the vastly different rates they develop from physical, physiological, emotional, and cognitive perspectives. From my own coaching experiences, I have witnessed many youngsters when they reach their mid-teenage years suddenly transcend in respect to their physical stature, emotional resilience, and responsibility for learning. It seems they have developed from being teenagers to young adults in a very short period. However, on the other hand I have witnessed youngsters take longer to reach full maturation; each individual is totally unique in this respect. Nature does not take short-cuts.

Due to the discrepancy in each child's rate of development, it is logical to expect performance levels to waver from time to time. However, many parents still often become concerned about where their child stands in comparison to other children, or become alarmed about a short-term decline in their child's performance level. This is understandable, but focusing on these two aspects can be a significant waste of time and emotional energy, and can often result in negative repercussions for everyone involved; particularly the child. The varying rates of maturation will invariably influence a young athlete's performance level; this is a perfectly natural process to expect. The 'Winning Parent' is able to appreciate the fact that their child's performance level will most likely fluctuate during their formative years due to variations in maturation rates; yet they are still able to uphold a patient and realistic outlook which acts as a bedrock of support for their child.

Empathy

Lauren Quigley:

"I feel that I was a bit lucky in that my mother had been an international swimmer herself. From early on she was good at knowing what it takes to really make it at swimming and what to avoid. For example, when I was 12 years old, she knew that I only needed to train twice a week whereas my coach wanted me there six days a week. She knew about burnout and stress, so she told the coach to step back from pushing me too hard. Lots of my friends did it, and at the time I wanted to do six days myself, but now they've all stopped swimming."

Adam Henley:

"I think it's a fine line when you're young between getting positive praise and negative criticism. It's not always easy because kids are different but you've got try and find a way to sail through the middle, between positivity and realistic feedback. Those that are always negative have no chance of helping. My parents did really well at finding a good balance with me. They never put pressure on me to achieve, they just gave me room to be myself really. Dave (my stepdad) has always been brilliant with me giving good constructive advice. He always gave me some ideas where I could improve in the form of a conversation with me, he never took it upon himself to make negative comments."

Scott Fitzgerald:

> *"You get lots of tough times, especially in boxing. It's really hard and that is when your family are really important to you. I couldn't do it if I felt that I was letting them down or if they got upset because I lost. I know they support me no matter what happens and that is a really big advantage to have growing up. You're doing it for yourself without added pressure yet when you win you can go and share it with them in a nice way. My parents know it's hard, and with my father being a boxer himself he knows the ups and downs personally!"*

People don't care how much you know until they know how much you care

Perhaps the most helpful emotional competency is the ability to empathize. Empathy is the basis of being able to accurately understand where another person is coming from emotionally and behaviorally. The power of this is extraordinary because feeling understood and listened to is a basic human need. Without it understanding will collapse, with it understanding will flow.

A bit of brain science: 'Love leads to empathy'

Having a connection with somebody else can be mapped in the brain. It is called limbic resonance. The brain's 'love center' lights up and releases the neurotransmitter's oxytocin and dopamine. Oxytocin and dopamine are fantastic natural drugs that promote feelings of harmony, love, and empathy. Consequently, when a person receives information from somebody they have 'limbic resonance' with, there is far more chance of a positive outcome. So in all close relationship situations the bond (limbic resonance) is very important. A parent can settle a child emotionally and relax them simply with a look and provide more energy by being around them.

The concept was advanced in the book <u>A General Theory of Love</u>[74], and is one of three interrelated concepts central to the book's premise: That our brain chemistry and nervous systems are measurably affected by those closest to us (limbic resonance); that our systems synchronize with one another in a way that has profound implications for personality and lifelong emotional health (limbic regulation); and that these set patterns can be modified through therapeutic practice (limbic revision).

Simply stated, this is why it is difficult to laugh at a joke told by a person you do not like, yet the same joke is hilarious from someone you connect with and already decided to be amusing.

The reversal of this is when the bond is lacking; the love missing, then stress related chemicals are released from the brain. People find it much harder to learn and perform in stress related states. So rather than being productive and helpful to a youngster, the parent actually harms the performance and learning by sending stress signals. The environment becomes negative underneath the surface, and as time goes on the parent-child interaction can become counterproductive as real enjoyment and fun disappears. The magic has gone.

It is impossible not to communicate – body language, silence, facial expression, gestures, gaze, posture, eye contact, tone and pace of voice; it all leaks out. Children learn when they are babies all these subtle ways to read you and your body language. They recognize your emotions and feelings before they can even talk. They still can!

So to them you are an open book, easy to read and they can easily pick up what you are actually feeling about them. They can look over to the sidelines and with just one glance read how you are feeling. You do not have to say you are disappointed for them to pick it up. You can't hide your panic if that's what you feel inside. They may not be able to articulate it themselves and you have the defense that, "I never said I was angry," but it's there. It is felt. The same goes for genuine pride and care. They can look at you and know you are loving, understanding, and happy for them. They know you are steady, in perspective and they can feel your pride in the limbic feelings they are getting. Yes, there is more to being a person's 'rock' than just saying you are.

Key message - You must be authentic!

You have to genuinely sit there watching them perform in a state of love and support and this comes easier when you have empathy for their situation. You understand their predicament more and ease off in your judgements. You see the innocence more clearly and find a place inside yourself where you are simply happy that they are healthy, trying, and dealing with life as best as they can with the tools they have. Then you just let the brain chemicals do their magic!

Joke time: A lack of empathy

A priest, a doctor, and an engineer were golfing one morning behind a particularly slow group of golfers.

The engineer fumed, ***"What's with those guys? We must have been waiting for fifteen minutes!"***

The doctor chimed in, ***"I don't know, but I've never seen such inept golf!"***

The priest said, ***"Here comes the greens keeper. Let's have a word with him."***

He said, ***"Hello, George. What's wrong with that group ahead of us? They're rather slow, aren't they?"***

The greens keeper replied, ***"Oh, yes. That's a group of blind firemen. They lost their sight saving our clubhouse from a fire last year, so we let them play for free anytime."***

The group fell silent for a moment. Then the priest said, ***"That's so sad. I think I'll say a special prayer for them."***

The doctor added, ***"Good idea. And maybe I could examine them to see if there's anything I can do for them."***

They were silent for a moment.

Then the engineer said, ***"Why can't they play at night?"***

Jokes are great because they can reveal some awkward truths in the cloak of humor. In this case we are reminded that although factually correct and in logical sense too, there is a time and a place for the truth. We are amused at the lack of empathy from the engineer, particularly in light of the priest's and doctor's responses. In the mind of the engineer, he has proposed a credible solution but the humor is he has missed the point (the need for empathy), as opposed to the other two not finding a solution to their delayed golf round.

I cringe at some of the times I have behaved like the engineer in this joke. There have been many occasions with my wife where after losing a match, I have been straight in there with the logical reasons and accusations that would have fixed the result. Thank goodness I have been able reduce this to almost zero and move much more towards sympathy in those early moments after disappointment. It took me quite a few years though I must say.

One of the biggest things that has helped me is my push to improve my own playing level and still compete at my own upper limits. There is nothing like going through an experience of your own, to appreciate some of the difficulties that exist. Sitting in our armchairs casting opinions on sport has practically become a hobby in itself. We see many pundits on TV and in the media doing it; why wouldn't we just join in too? It is only when you get up and get playing yourself again, dealing with a sport and its pressures, that you are reminded your 'armchair theories' do not always stack up so well. There is nothing like a good defeat to put me back firmly into the land of empathy as I am reminded of all the challenges of competing at the edge of your limits. I know I am a better coach when this happens too. I think an excerpt from the 'Citizenship in a Republic' speech delivered by Theodore Roosevelt delivered in Paris (in 1910) summarizes this sentiment well:

> *"It is not the critic who counts; not the man who points out how the strong man stumbles, or where the doer of deeds could have done them better. The credit belongs to the man who is actually in the arena, whose face is marred by dust and sweat and blood; who strives valiantly; who errs, who comes short again and again, because there is no effort without error and shortcoming; but who does actually strive to do the deeds; who knows great enthusiasms, the great devotions; who spends himself in a worthy cause; who at the best knows in the end the triumph of high achievement, and who at the worst, if he fails, at least fails while daring greatly, so that his place shall never be with those who neither know victory nor defeat."[75]*

"The older I get, the better I was!"

I love this saying. I love dropping it in with all my mates and those parents that talk about how they used to deal with pressured sport. The "good old days" where "we just got on with it didn't we!" A time when "players were tough" and when "you didn't need a psychologist." Mutual backslapping and selective memories are glorified and repeated to the point where in your own mind you genuinely were a sporting great, who with a bit of luck could have met professional standards.

Naturally, it is nice to reminisce, and who would deprive people of those warming memories, even if they are a slightly exaggerated! The serious point however is that some people do forget what a struggle competitive sport can be. Trapped in a haze of memory induced bliss, empathy can be clouded over and this does no good for anyone; especially the children on the receiving end of such inflated viewpoints.

So my tip here is to get out and compete at something important to you now. No matter what your age or standard, go out and remind yourself just how hard life is in the moment of challenging sports competition. Go to your next level up, not just the one you are comfortable at. Try the level where you experience the physical demands, the emotional mind games, the mistakes that come out of nowhere, and the observers judging you. Feel the embarrassment after a mistake, the frustration of your opponent controlling you, or the tendency to look for excuses when you fail. Notice how your practice level often dips down when you compete under a bit of pressure and laugh at how your pre-match tactics are unraveled by your cunning opponent. Then become aware of how you start to fear the sport at that level, and how your overall confidence begins to ebb away. You will become acutely aware of the reality check that is taking place. Notice the allure of dropping back to that little comfy pond you used to swim in, and also notice how sensitive you start to become to small criticisms and jokes at your failings.

If you want to take it a step further, give your parents a call. Yes, ask them to come along if they can make it, to watch your progress. Session in and session out, have them sit there as you struggle on the battlefield and notice how your emotions change. Afterwards, invite them to comment on your efforts, notice how you react.

This wouldn't be for everyone of course, but hopefully you get the point I am trying to articulate. Just imagining this can give you empathy, but taking part in a sporting activity/event really does hit home this point. I have this to this day with my dad: He watches me play squash at the highest level I can still push. Luckily for me, he has never pressured me at sport and I simply feel inspiration; yet if he ever does criticize you can bet it doesn't help much!

Empathy builders

- *Go and watch the Disney Pixar movie 'Inside Out'[76]. Simple really; just go and watch it.*

- *Get out and compete just out of your comfort zone, with a crowd watching. It will help you personally and it will certainly build empathy.*

- *Learn a new skill yourself. Go and be a beginner or improver again.*

Humility

"To truly accept one's own powerlessness is liberating. Whenever I feel like I am spoiled and I want more than I deserve, I try to refocus myself

and remember growing up. That puts things back in perspective. I remember the things that I really value: family, fun, joy, happiness, love. We have a saying in our country. Whenever nothing hurts, put a stone in your shoe, and start walking. Always have that in your mind, because you are aware of the hardships others face."[77]

Novak Djokovic, World Number One - Men's Tennis

Throughout my research the one word that has come up more than any other is the word **humility**. It seems that being **humble** is one of the major ingredients to becoming a 'Winning Parent'.

The definition of humility: *The quality or condition of being <u>humble</u>; modest opinion or estimate of one's own importance and rank.*

John Trower interview

My interview with John Trower, from the University of Central Lancashire, was particularly illuminating in respect to the value of being humble.

Me: You have talked a lot about humility and in particular how parents and coaches require lots of it. Can you explain what you mean?

John: *I believe a person's upbringing is so important. At the time you don't know what is going on or how important it is in affecting the rest of your life. One of the absolute core things is that adults have rank over the children. Parents rule and lead while the youngsters follow. Children need to know that they must go through things they don't want to. In my youth, Saturday was sport day which was brilliant, but Sunday was for singing in the church choir, visiting relatives, and family life. I hated Sundays because all I wanted to do was play sport, but my mother in particular was not to be crossed on these issues. It made us learn to deal with things we did not necessarily want to do. We learned how to tolerate these things and in some cases realize there was an occasional upside by going with it. Yes it's bad we have to visit Aunt Mary all afternoon, but we may get one of her nice cakes at the end. We may have to sing in the church and go to choir practice, but it will be a good feeling when we perform as a team at Easter Mass or something. This is how you learn humility, to understand your place in the pecking order, and how to behave accordingly. There will be a better time later on, but for now you must follow our lead and get through things you don't want to do.*

This is the critical thing that all the best performers I have worked with have in abundance. Becoming a successful performer in sport requires a huge ability to put yourself through things you would not want to go through by choice. Yet you do it because there are better times to come. It shows up hugely when performers go through tough phases of training and competitive challenges. If you have humility you accept that tough days must be worked through, and that you need to accept some home truths from your coaches. You have the quality of respecting rank and getting back in the pecking order quickly. You accept criticism more easily and can take on the responsibility to meet the next challenge which sport and life will always throw at you. Basically, you can find a way to deal with it and fix it.

Me: So humility as you say contributes to their toughness?

John: *It is the basis of their resilience! It is the heart of their ability to keep coming back for more. They can take defeats more easily and very importantly, not get too carried away after victory. It is like Saturday and Sunday, good days and not so good days! Part of life!*

I am convinced this quality is embedded in our youth by parents. In my opinion it can always be pinned down to the discipline set down by the parents in a person's youth, sometimes by the mother or sometimes by the Father; but one of them has to be strong. A child will learn very quickly where they don't want to go with their parents and how not to waste their time and resources. The message being laid down is, "do things properly, with enthusiasm or don't do them at all because I haven't the time or money to waste on you." It is hard at first, but the rewards come later in life because you have taught the child humility.

Me: I get a feeling that more and more children are becoming the ones at the top of the pecking order. They are the center of more conversations, and they are given so much support and help. Most concerning though, I notice how much control they have on their parent's emotions. The child knows they've got them worrying about them.

John: *I agree. There is no doubt times have changed. When life is tough and many hours must be worked to make ends meet, there is an element of basic survival that infiltrates the family. There is no luxury of time to overdo the fussing of children; you're too busy getting by and getting the basics in place. With more financial freedom and more time on people's hands, we have seen a boom in increased coaching and support and less discipline in terms of kids* *being made to do things they don't want to do, such as Sunday school or tedious family outings! A decrease in humility!*

Me: Generally speaking, I suppose children are much less bored nowadays with all the gadgets, with social media, games and media platforms. They are forever entertained; there is always the option out.

John: *That is a good point. Humility comes through suffering a bit and getting through it regularly. I suppose a two-hour car journey, or a period of time in your room isn't quite the same misery as it used to be!*

Rafael Nadal

For me, the stand out autobiography I have read for how parents and family have influenced a performer's level of humility is Rafael Nadal's. It is no accident that Rafael is abundantly humble, amazing at tennis, and the ultimate warrior out on the tennis court. In his book he says:

"It is true my uncle did a lot to build that fighting character but my values as a person and my way of being, which ultimately underlie my game, come from my father and mother. They were proper about things like table manners and the need to be courteous and polite to everybody. My mother says that if I were not, if I behaved like a spoiled brat, she would still love me, but she would be too embarrassed to travel half way around the world to watch me play.

They drummed into me the importance of treating everybody with respect from an early age. Whenever we lost a football [soccer] match, my father insisted that I had to go up to the players of the other team and congratulate them. I had to say to each one of them something like, "Well done champ. Very well played," I didn't like it. I felt miserable when we lost, and my face must have shown that my heart wasn't in the words I was saying. But I knew I'd get into trouble if I didn't do as my father said, so I did it. And the habit stayed with me. It comes naturally to me to praise my opponent after he's beaten me."[78]

The Karate Kid: A lesson in humility!

For me, the immensely popular and iconic movie 'The Karate Kid'[79] encapsulates the issue of humility superbly. Most of us likely recall that in this movie the protagonist is a teenager named Daniel LaRusso and he is being bullied by a group of individuals practicing an illegal form of karate, 'Cobra Kai'. This victimization only ceases when Mr. Miyagi (a karate tutor and Daniel's apartment complex' maintenance guy) intervenes by turning the tables on this group of attackers.

Following this episode, in order for Daniel to defend himself and prepare for a karate tournament in which he will face this group of bullies, Mr. Miyagi agrees to teach him a form of karate. It is during the early stages of Daniel's training that is particularly meaningful. He is instructed to paint garden fences, wax cars, and carry out other seemingly trivial chores. It is a painful experience for Daniel, and he finds it difficult to cope with. It all comes to a head when Daniel aggressively accuses Mr. Miyagi of treating him inappropriately; he believes the menial chores served absolutely no purpose whatsoever. He couldn't understand why Mr. Miyagi would treat him like this!

However, Daniel soon realized there was in fact a 'method behind the madness' in relation to Mr. Miyagi's thinking. Daniel was firmly informed that spending hours 'grooving' the correct technique of a brush stroke or waxing a car hood would enhance muscle memory; and in turn this would be amazingly beneficial for the execution of karate skills and techniques. But although Daniel had to perform these tedious duties under the purpose of technical development, there were also other pertinent reasons for his being subjected to these tasks. He was teaching Daniel life skills.

First, it taught him the art of patience. Mr. Miyagi preached to Daniel that he couldn't rush these tasks if he wished to complete them in an effective manner. But more pertinently for me, it was a stark lesson in **humility**. Mr. Miyagi was exposing Daniel to the actualities of life; he was making him acutely aware that to become a humble human being, sometimes he had to do things he didn't actually want to do. He was also showing Daniel his place in the pecking order, making sure that he didn't rise too far above his station and become too arrogant. He was ensuring Daniel learned how to stay resilient when things got tough. The message of this movie resonates with me far more today than it did 30 years ago; I now appreciate the powerful message is conveys. Although the movie includes scenes of violence, teenage romance, and an epic comeback, there is no question the **lesson of humility** is the standout theme!

I asked Lauren Quigley about humility

Me: Have your parents kept you level headed Lauren?

Lauren Quigley: *Yes, I'd like to think so. My brother swims a lot too and he wouldn't let me get carried away. My parents are quite happy in life anyway,* *they do their own thing well. They are proud of me and get nervous watching me and all that, but they don't go round showing off about what I've done with my swimming so far.*

Me: Have you seen other young competitive swimmers struggle to keep their humility when they've had success?

Lauren Quigley: *Yes, a lot. I see a lot of other families buzzing too much off success. It can be over the top. I've seen other swimmers quit because when they were younger they made the Olympic team, and they all thought, "I've made it." Everyone got carried away. They've quit now because they feel like failures. You've got to be proud, but you can't become a show-off and neither can your family.*

Growing up to be humble is no accident. Understanding your place in society and learning to 'take your medicine' when life is there to teach you a lesson is a quality that parents must work skillfully to instill. Coaches, schoolteachers, and grandparents can all reinforce this, as Bryan Jones outlined in 'The Doctor and the Academic' earlier in the book when he discussed 'stability zones.' Yet it appears to me from my research, and my own repeated observations, that where there is a humble and balanced sports person there is at least one mighty humble parent just in the shadows. A parent who has been centered, who has reinforced boundaries and standards of human etiquette, and who themselves continue to remain humble.

Usain and LeBron

Basketball star LeBron James and sprinting legend Usain Bolt are known for their skills and accomplishments, and loved for their humility. Here are two quotes that suggest why:

LeBron James on his mother:

"Being a mother - it's the toughest job in the world. It's tougher than being a professional athlete or being the president. It's a powerful thing. I had my mother to blanket me, to give me security. [When I was] growing up, she was my mother, my father, everything. To grow up in a single-parent household and see what she could do all by herself that gave me a lot of strength."[80]

Norman Peart (Usain Bolt's Manager) speaking about Usain's parents:

"I go out of my way with Usain, always because his parents trusted me with him when he was just 16 years old. His parents call me 'Mr. Peart', even though his dad is old enough to be my dad. His parents and I have the same values, and since then, there is hardly a day that we have not been in touch. For me, it has been the support of his parents that has made Usain what he is today. There is a very close relationship between that family – parents, brother, and sister. That's where Usain's strength is."[81]

Summary

Be a Co-pilot: Like all good co-pilots, you are highly skilled, supportive, calming, and you exude confidence in yourself and the pilot.

Patience: Although it is very difficult, if you can learn to add to your patience great rewards will come down the line.

There really is no such thing as a **Professional Junior** - they are simply children who perform and play sport. Always remember this premise.

Empathy: Remember your love for them and understand some of the difficulties of sport and the pressure it can bring.

Humility: Work skillfully to keep them humble: humble with other people, humble with the sport itself, and humble with their achievements.

Notes & Reminders

Flight Path: Stage 6

'Get Doing – Now!'

Stage 6: Fly High and Far 'Get Doing – Now!'

Time to do!

If you want to fly high and far, there is no other way around it but to get to work on making changes. Here we are talking about how you handle the practical moments before, during, and after competitions. You want improved sport parenting habits, so that even on tougher days you are still very effective.

What are we going to look at?

1. How to be better in the build up to competitions.
2. How to be more effective when watching your children compete.
3. How to react in the best way after the competition has ended.

Specifically, we will look at issues such as:

- The car ride to and from the competitions.
- Your relationship with their coaches.
- Coping with your nerves and excitement.
- Processing disappointment and victory.
- Dealing with what others think of you as you begin to grow.
- Sticking to your 'winning definition' under pressure.

Habits are even stronger than reason

To improve at doing anything requires a sustained and focused effort. Once we continue this, we form a **habit.** Habits remain one of the most powerful psychological forces; our brains are designed to repeat patterns that have been fed into it. The more we feed a particular movement, thought process, emotion, or all 3 combined, our brains will automatically and easily reproduce it. **The brain does not know what a good habit or a bad habit is.** It simply wants to repeat behaviors and thinks that it gets used to being fed by you.

Lying in bed every morning until 10am and then getting up at 7am one day will send your body into shock. It will be much more difficult to get up if the habit is getting up at 10am. If after a few weeks you have repeatedly gotten up at 7am every day, suddenly you will actually struggle to stay in bed until 10am. Neither is a good habit or a bad habit; it just is what it is.

Sports parent habits

Each time you watch your child **compete**, you go through the same rituals and your habits come through.

Here are 3 examples: If you had to pick from **Parent (A), (B), or (C)** which one is most typically like you, and which would you choose?

Parent (A) - Competition day arrives and you are feeling nervous. You consider not watching because you tend to lose control even though you know it isn't a good thing. You have a quick word with yourself and decide to watch, expecting that today is the day you will keep it all together. You sit or stand in the usual place (usually among other parents where you can be seen and heard) and you set off intent that today is the day you will be calm and in the mood not to criticize or judge them. The competition starts and slowly you feel yourself breathing a bit quicker. The score becomes more important. Suddenly the opposition are more annoying and their coach and supporters irritate to you. Out of nowhere you start shouting encouragement which turns into instructions. Next thing you know you are making gestures and your facial expressions are all over the place. You manage to get a hold of your child's attention, and yet again it's like you're in the competition yourself. Needless to say, win or lose, you have lots to comment on after the competition has finished. On the way home you are not shy of an argument and even a few threats of withdrawal if your child doesn't improve soon. Passive aggression can take over you as you ramp up the silent treatment and stay stuck in an internal dark mood. If a win occurs, the predominant feelings are of power, of assurance in your convictions, and of relief for the child. *"We showed them didn't we?"*

Parent (B) - Competition day arrives and you are looking forward to spending a day with your daughter. You don't know much about the event itself, just the times, venue, and name of the opposition. Competition time arrives and you say good luck to your child, tell them you love them, and then you go away and listen to your favorite music or go and sit with friends. You have three reminders of how you want to handle today's experience written on a piece of paper or on your phone.

Examples:

1. *I love watching my daughter play and it is always a privilege.*

2. *Sit up straight, breathe deeply when you can, and try to smile where you can.*

3. *If you feel the stress coming and the panic, take five deep breaths and think about how hard it is out there for them.*

You read these examples quietly somewhere while imagining yourself behaving this way. You phone a good friend or text a nice message to someone you love, then go and watch your daughter compete. You generally remain calm throughout the completion of the event, and despite very much wanting your daughter to be victorious, you keep a bigger perspective, and whatever the result you still behave as if you love her immediately after the match. On the way home you are quite consistent, no matter what the result. Without much analysis of the match, when your daughter wants to let off steam or celebrate, you listen and join in as you see fit. You are quite good at moving on to new matters in your day without much resistance. Life moves on, 'c'est la vie' as the French say. Sometimes your daughter calls you her 'rock.'

Parent (C) - Competition day approaches and you feel yourself planning and getting ready for your support duties. You ask what needs preparing the day before and make sure you do everything asked of you. Dietary needs correct, kit bag ready, travel times organized, opponents studied, all bases covered. In the car ride to the competition you tell your son what you expect to happen and how he needs to prepare and compete. You almost feel like you are competing yourself. You believe you will make a significant difference to your son today in how he performs and also the result of it. Competition starts and inside you are as pumped as the performers. You get involved immediately, supporting and offering instructions. You are cheering and supporting when they do well, shouting at them or looking displeased when panicking (though you don't know you are panicking). The result is all that matters today, and after the performance is finished everyone can tell the result by looking at how you are behaving. A win, and all is well with the world, friendly and high as a kite; a loss, and you are miserable looking for the exit and somewhere to wallow. Either way, on the way home it is hard for you to stay calm, even harder to resist your post-match breakdown of the referee's performance, your child's display, the opposition, and the coach's decisions. You take quite a bit of responsibility for the performance yourself and therefore view the relationship with your child as a team. **'We'** will fix this, no time to lose. More coaching, more practice, more planning. This can't happen again. 'Onwards and upwards' you profess, and only settle once your child has agreed to the plan.

Clearly these are generalizations, and maybe you have a mixture; but maybe you can recognize yourself in one of them more than in the others. It would be very difficult to move from the actions and behavior of parent (C) to (B) in your habits or (B) to (C). As to what is effective, there are elements in all three that can help or hinder, with much depending on your own individual situation and definition of winning. The key point is to find a way that works and not to get stuck in one fixed and typical reaction. Be flexible in your approaches and reactions as you go along the journey.

Be flexible

"Anyone can become angry – that is easy. But to be angry with the right person, to the right degree, at the right time, for the right purpose, and in the right way – that is not easy."[82]

Aristotle

I love the concept of **Ashby's Law of Requisite Variety**. Ross Ashby was an English psychiatrist and a pioneer in cybernetics, the study of **complex systems**. Now I doubt Ashby was specifically relating to the complexity of being a sports parent back in 1956, but I am sure he would appreciate the complexity of parenting combined with competition and therefore this equates to his theory. Ashby proposed that: ***The element of any system that has more flexibility will tend to have more control within that system.***[83]

A good example of this is the wise and experienced parent who has understood the phrase 'there is more than one way to skin a cat.' They have a number of approaches on how to handle situations and this gives them ultimate control. Like the grandmaster chess player who can adapt his strategy mid-game or the football coach who can choose the correct lineup of players to fit a certain condition, the greater the flexibility the more chance of a win.

You can improve your parenting flexibility by trying fresh approaches and widening your habits. You will have options of how to react to situations you find yourself encountering. You will have greater positive influence on your child's development by having a wider array of appropriate skills and emotional control. You will not be so easy to be 'wound up' by your children, nor will you feel as inadequate when they begin their clever little rebellions against you. The flipside is summed up again perfectly by the words of *Abraham Maslow*: **"I suppose it is tempting, if the only tool you have is a hammer, to treat everything as if it were a nail".**[84]

I have noticed parents who can only shout to motivate, who can only bellow instructions to teach, and can only talk of solutions when they are asked to listen. There is no change in their approach week after week. They believe the only way to be is their way. 'It worked for me, it will work for you,' type of logic. Well this may work in a simple system, but in a complicated and ever changing environment as is the competitive sports journey, they will eventually lose control to those that have the power of flexible options.

Task: Think of a competitive sports situation with your child where you believe you acted in the following ways

You acted in a rash manner:

You made your child relax and helped them look forward to the challenge ahead:

You allowed your ego to get in the way:

You compared your child to other children or to another child's performance:

You displayed overbearing tendencies:

You recognized a moment or situation where what you were going to say, or the way you were going to act, would have a negative effect, so you stopped yourself:

You did something out of the ordinary. For example, you sat in the car and missed the majority of the game as you were talking to your relative on the phone:

All these approaches have value but the most successful ones will be most appropriate because they are aligned with your definition of winning and your personal circumstances.

Inertia – don't stay stuck, gain momentum!

British physicist Sir Isaac Newton's first law includes the term 'Inertia.' Put simply he proposed: **"Every object will remain at rest or continue with uniform motion unless it is acted upon by an unbalanced force."**[85]

In simpler terms, inertia means: Something that's moving will stay moving and something that is stuck will stay stuck, until there is an outside effort to stop it or start it.

To get going in the first place will require a big effort because your brain is trained to stay as you are. Old habits die hard. But the good news is that **"Once you get going you are hard to stop." You will have momentum**

The rule is therefore clear. If you desire any permanent change to your existing habits you will need to put in a lot of effort at first. This could be determined effort that must last for weeks or even months. Your habits will be ingrained in you at different depths so some won't take much effort compared to others. For example, I would expect it will be far easier to say one or two more positive comments at your child's next competitive event, than it will be to overcome the nerves that have been pervading your pre-game rituals for years.

Consider your habits and rituals that affect your sports parenting experience.

- *What do you usually say to your children before they compete?*
- *Where do you watch from?*
- *Who do you watch with?*
- *What frame of mind do you normally end up in?*
- *Are your current habits helping?*
- *Can you be flexible in what you do or are you stuck?*
- *How many times are you willing to try something to gain momentum?*
- *Do you need help from anyone in particular?*

TODAY is the time!

Habits are very much about now, this moment, today! I see many people setting long-term goals which are rather exciting but too comfortable. They usually require effort tomorrow or next week. Tomorrow never comes for many people as we know.

- **Get moving today by changing one thinking habit and just one behavior habit. Stick with it.**

- **If you can do that, then and only then should you consider setting some long-term goals.**

- **Prove to yourself you can do something to change TODAY. After a few weeks of this, you will have the confidence and belief to be doing new things.**

John Trower talking about how reflection leads to deliberateness

Me: What have the best parents been good at when working with you?

John: *The ones who reflect are. People who are good at reflecting on their own decisions and behaviors tend to show progress. Parents who are always up for that, seem to do well because they move with the times while retaining some of their own key values. They have asked me good questions regarding their parenting decisions because they want to talk and improve on what they are doing. For example, they may ask,* **"do you think I am too intense with Sarah?"** *or* **"would it be helpful if I came and watched the coaching session or stayed away a little more?"**

Better parents can clearly reflect on their own upbringing and pick out the parts that really helped them in the long-term, something they could only appreciate in hindsight. This helps them realize the bigger picture and then it is easier for them to change or keep going with certain things.

I think what helps leadership skills overall is when parents have an ongoing enthusiasm to learn and improve. I very much believe in **'reflection leads to deliberateness'.** *If you reflect and you believe that your current 'default setting' needs changing then you must actually make attempts to change.* **So by thinking and reflecting, a person is only half way there; they must commit to changing their behaviors.** *This may be a parent enforcing rules where previously they were too soft, or it could be giving their children more space rather than smothering them and over-analyzing.*

Me: Yes. So if a parent reflects that they are getting too stressed and too involved with their child's sport and realize that the space they were given as a child really helped them in the long run, they have actually got to do something about it.

John: *Yes, like staying away from a few performances for a while or finding a new way to talk to them. I suppose whatever works really for that situation.*

Me: It seems quite a basic thing doesn't it?

John: *It is! That is the thing, it is a simple concept. That doesn't mean it's easy to implement though, because as a parent you always tend to think you're doing nothing wrong because it's usually in good faith.*

Me: That is exactly what I went through with my wife. It was only when I reflected and had a kind of 'epiphany' moment that I realized I needed to take a back seat and change what I was doing.

John: *Yes, and the best people do this without holding a grudge or behaving like a victim about it. They are happy to change because it helps the process for everyone.*

Handling change - What will others think of me?

A common blockage to changing what we do is thinking we need to keep consistent with what other people expect of us. Because of this, at times it's almost as if many of us are cocooned in a prison of limitation. Generally we want to behave with what fits our own personality expectations and what we believe others expect of us. It's like it's more important to be you than to change and get different results. What will people think? Maybe they'll be saying, *"What has happened to big Al? He's gone soft all of a sudden, after everything he said about being tough and getting involved."* Or maybe people will think, *"Look at Sarah's mother sitting on her own, listening to her music. Who does she think she is?"*

If you decide to change and try out new things in your sports parenting approach, **do not worry about what other people think**. Often, they do not want you to be different; they prefer you to be steady and obvious. In some ways we think someone who is steady is a person you can rely on. You know your place and that you are liked by others if you stay that way. So a big thing is that you have to expect that some people will resent you for experimenting with new ideas. It will scare them a little and rather than admiring your strength they will criticize what they see as your inconsistency. They may even call you a faker!

The main person you have to convince though is yourself. If you want to believe in yourself and your ability to change and grow, you must be prepared to visualize yourself doing new things and having success by doing so. You can't afford to think, "I tried it but it's not really me that, is it?" or "I just can't stand by and watch other people beating my son; I just have to help him fix it. It's what I do at work; it's what my family have always done!"

Ultimately, these identity beliefs will be the thing that holds you back in the face of committing to new action. Most people I have worked with do not give new behaviors the chance to bed into their nervous systems. They try once or twice and then quite happily self-sabotage or panic, and revert right back to a place of comfort which is their current self-identity. I hear some parents telling me, ***"Yes, I've tried that Danny and it doesn't really work with my daughter; she just went the other way and ignored me. I think I will just see how it goes; I think she will grow out of it. I used to be just like her you know."*** I want to ask: How many times did you try? How did you reinforce your new behavior and ride the inevitable protest from your daughter? How did you try and adapt the new approach so you found a better solution than, *"I hope she grows out of it"?*

As a coach however, I have learned not to push these parents too hard with their reasoning. These are the questions I can push the performers with, but it can be a leap too far for many parents. Saying this, there are those parents who welcome the challenge and in the interests of their own progression will step out of their comfort zone and stick to new ideas until they make them work.

Example of repeated action:

A Canadian father contacted me after reading some of the tweets I posted on @winningparent. After chatting over Skype for an hour or so, we came up with a three-point plan that he would follow during his son's ice hockey game days. It revolved around the car journey to the competition, during play, and the car journey home. We came up with very simple things, some of which are in the suggestions discussed in this stage of the book. He committed to trying it for one month, which meant five competitions. I didn't hear back from him until about five weeks later. I had forgotten all about it when I picked up a voicemail from him:

"Hey Danny, Bill here. I just wanted to let you know how much you've helped me with my son. Things are going great, we feel like friends again. He is even laughing at my jokes. I realized I don't need him to be doing anything much to make me love him more. Watching from a calmer place let me see how much he was trying his best, and how all the kids on the ice were going for it too. I had got so carried away about this stuff, I couldn't see it was just sport. I look forward to taking him now and we have a routine going each game. Ok - that's it I guess, just wanted to let you know. Let's talk soon! Thanks."

Example of Staying Stuck:

One lovely parent I worked with last year highlighted very clearly that the way she viewed herself prevented making changes to the way she related with her son. She said:

"I really understand what you are saying, I really do get it. It is better when I stay strong after the abuse he gives me, I actually felt good doing it and felt proud but I can't continue to keep doing it. He loves his sport and I think he may not play if I keep challenging his behavior. It is just the way he is. I don't think I have the strength to do it. I could never forgive myself if he quit."

After she said this to me, I knew there was no point continuing my work with her. I knew I was up against deep rooted self-doubt and limitations. Until this lady worked on her own beliefs and self-esteem, there was no way her behaviors could go to the place they needed to go in order to deal with the challenge of her son's anger and abuse.

I was not about to cause more confusion and push her further into despair. A person must realize they need to think differently about themselves and commit to new responses if they want new results. At this time, this mother was not ready to make the leap into committed action. We remain friends, and she is slowly acquiring more awareness of her need to change her own limiting beliefs if she wants to lead her son in a different way.

The three key times of action

Although it is important that you can help your children around competition time, you do not need to be 'treading on eggshells' here; that type of hypersensitivity can be just as damaging as overdoing it. Just aim to be there as a support through all the phases, and over time work out what works best and what needs eliminating. It is an evolving process, not a stuck set of rules.

The first key time of action: The build-up to competition. Be aware!

This can be any time or moment before competition, weeks, days, hours, or minutes. There can be a tendency to over fuss in the build-up to competition. I would suggest keeping things as normal as possible. Showing that life goes on as normal before a performance can take pressure away, and it communicates that you aren't nervous either. Suddenly treating them like royalty or pandering to their anxieties can simply add to the perceived importance of sports competition.

When my wife won the world championships in Penang, Malaysia we had begun a habit of taking it in turns to go to Starbucks in the afternoon to get drinks. On the day she was competing in the tournament final, it was Laura's turn to go and get the drinks. People couldn't believe that when just three hours before the biggest match of her life, she came round the pool delivering me my Frappuccino for the day as I lay sunbathing.

The worst thing I could have done was to say, "oh no, you must not go today because your match is so important." It would just have added more hype to an already tense occasion. Here are some suggestions that can be implemented during the build-up to competition:

Refrain from asking questions that you wouldn't normally ask, such as:

- **Have you eaten enough?**
- **How did you sleep?**
- **You're quiet today: What's up?**

- **Do you think you are going to win today?**
- **Do you feel good?**

Just like before finals (exams) at school, be careful not to ask your children questions that they can't directly answer with proof. To you it may feel like a good conversation starter, to them it makes you sound insensitive to their plight. Instead, leave the questions to them or ask practical questions that have a logical answer, such as: **What time would you like to be there today?**

Direct the topic of conversation onto your life or the life of others

This subtly reminds every one of the bigger picture of life. We can all become so wrapped up in our own little world that we create pressure that is out of proportion. Remembering what we're all part of and that others are facing their own challenges every day (some much harder than our own), can really bring a better sense of your own life circumstances. If nothing else, the change in focus allows breathing space for all concerned.

Allow silence

Silence can really help sometimes. Silence can allow a person to process their racing mind for themselves. Moments of silence can provide fantastic clarity and serenity; especially during stressful times. The phrase 'speech is sliver but silence is golden' wasn't conjured up for no reason!

Just Listen

Listening gives people a great chance to get things off their chests. Just allowing your children to vocalize their pre-performance stresses will be a big help to them. When they explain their worries this isn't always code for, "please will you fix my problems for me." Therefore, maybe say, "I hear you yes, it's tough isn't it? (Empathy) Do you want me to help with that or are you all set?"

Do not turn the car into a sport analysis suite

Just because your children have to listen because they're locked in with you does not mean it is time for you to turn into Mr. or Mrs. 'expert' sports pundit. Overall stick to a routine that works well for you; over time it pays off if they associate travelling in cars with relaxation, fun, privacy, and freedom as opposed to interrogation, stress, and boredom. If they want to discuss anything with you let them bring it up. Learn to trust them.

To carry or not to carry!

I've heard many experts fiercely criticize parents for carrying their children's bags and organizing their kit and equipment. For me it is a personal choice. Such things can be nice and normal things to do, or limiting. As long as there is clear appreciation and respect from the child to the parent, then who is anyone from the outside to say this is poor practice. The best approach may be to mix it up, and get them to carry your bags once in a while!

Your definition of winning (Stage 2):

Go over these key agreements before competition time and write them down. It will help you to get on the same page as your child again because it is easy to forget. How you define success will give you clear benchmarks of how you can win today, despite what the scoreboard says. Coaches call this 'performance focus' as opposed to 'results focus'. Of course you can strive for both at once, but usually focusing on performance accomplishments leads to desired results.

The second key time of action: During the competition - Be careful!

This is anytime from the start of their performance to the end: a time where they may look over to you, a time where you are in the 'hot-seat'. For most, this is the most emotional time! Some choose not to watch; it can be that overwhelming. Here you will show much of your feelings through body language, facial expressions, and gesturing. Some parents have explained to me it is the equivalent to the feeling of stepping onto a roller coaster and strapping in for the ride.

The mother of Andy Murray (Former Wimbledon, Olympic, and U.S Open Tennis Champion); Judy Murray says, *"When I am watching my boys compete it's like a mixture of nausea and a heart attack all going on at the same time, and it hasn't got any easier; it's actually got harder."*[86]

This is where you need to make sure you are keeping a useful perspective because it is so easy to get pulled into the drama. If your emotions go out of control then essentially you have gone into a panic state. Here are some suggestions that can help you avoid the overspill:

Buddy Up

Sit with a fellow parent and each time you notice each other going a little overboard or getting too emotional (e.g. angry, abusive, over instructive, over negative, disrespectful of opposition or officials, nervous), pass them an object you have agreed is a signal to 'wake up'. Earlier, Bryan Jones whom you met in 'The Doctor and the Academic' suggested a 'bean bag' to his clients, and he said it worked great. Being passed the object by a respected friend will at the very least distract you and break your state. It can also prove to be slightly amusing in the moment too!

Positive Mantra

Have a mantra or question you can say to yourself such as: "Above everything else, I love my child and today I hope he strives to meet his learning goals." This alone can bring huge relief as you begin to think of things like health, love, and enjoyment. Your child can compete as hard as they want, but you can afford the luxury of understanding what this is all part of. You can understand the lessons they are going through are preparing them for the wider world, and that the basic joy of their sport participation should always be cherished.

What does your child prefer?

Ask your child what they want from you from the sidelines. Do they want you to be there at all? Do they want you to be quiet and just watch? Do they want you to be involved by helping with occasional instruction or support? Ask them if you distract them in any way and if they would like you to be a little different? How visible do they want you to be, close to the action or further away? It is always a good idea to ask these questions within a conversation and act on them accordingly. Some days they will need different things from you, so in my experience it is best not to leave it to guesswork. It also reminds them that they are responsible for their choices and that you are prepared to listen to them when they voice their opinions.

You are a human not a robot

Remember that you are not perfect and emotions will get the better of you much of the time. Let your child know this too. As long as they notice improvement and support they will benefit from your changes in approach. If you can start to feel your emotions building up and you're able to prevent them from dominating your responses, then you know you are heading in the right direction.

Practice your preferred posture

Your body language often influences your brain as much as the other way around too. Notice how lazy you feel when you slouch about all day, yet energized when you get up and get your body moving. Armies all through history have practiced posturing and marching a certain way to boost mental states and give off positive impressions. So if you like to be relaxed then practice what it feels like to sit relaxed for you. Get to know your breathing rate, where your hands sit, and how your face feels. If you want to be alert and attentive then practice this posture too. What is your head position? How do your shoulders feel and what type of gestures do you make? Some I know like to just work with their face, keeping a relaxed smile throughout a performance, others have learned to sit on their hands. One popular idea is to have something of comfort in your hands to occupy them or even chewing gum has helped many a nervous coach. Whatever works for you, practice it until you can trust it.

Use Apps or Music

There are many brilliant applications available to you on your phones these days. One of my favorites is called 'Headspace'. It is very simple to follow a ten minute exercise that is most helpful in calming down racing thoughts and emotions. It is like taking a brilliant power nap for the brain, and I have personally found it to be excellent for getting me into a much more appropriate state when I am supporting a player during performance.

Music has also been a big help to me just prior to and during performances. The great thing about music is that you can select the tunes that put you in a certain mood. Some are calm, some pump you up, and some inspire. Make a personal playlist and let the music help you along the ride. Another one is possibly listening to podcasts, particularly when someone is narrating with a nice relaxed tone. I know some recreational runners who follow this approach, and they have reported that they feel much calmer after listening to a relaxing podcast.

The third key time of action: After the competition - Be very careful!

In terms of competition and your behavior, this is the most important time of the three, as it is ***a hypersensitive moment for your child.*** Therefore, if you want to leave an impression on them this is the time to do it! But remember, this is also a crucial moment when they can really judge your character and true intentions. Here are some suggestions:

Not too high - not too low

Results in youth competitions can be important, but rarely are they more important than those in professional sport. I know the children can believe they are, and that is nice to see sometimes. It's good to witness children playing with passion and fighting as if the event is the most important thing. However, as the adults, we can help keep things in perspective. We are used to seeing the reactions of sports professionals on TV, who quite rightly are often extremely pleased after victory and desolate after defeat. You do not need to follow this direction. It is recommended you go down the middle more, and be a bastion of calm in their storm. Show them that your love is unconditional irrespective of the final result. You are pleased for them when they win, and you are sympathetic to their feelings when they lose. If they don't try or they behave outside of the agreed boundaries, then you should consistently assert your response.

It is up to parents in particular to keep the lid on things and prevent the 'all or nothing' culture that can creep into youngsters when they enter competitions. By all means encourage maximum effort, encourage desire to win, and remind them that the point of competition is to come out on top. But whatever the final result is, you should go about 'steadying the ship' in the proportionate way. I know how hard it can be to implement this sentiment; it takes strength and conviction to do so. But through practice, I have undoubtedly learned how beneficial it can be over the long-term.

Ask yourself this important question: What is important about how I handle this in the long-term? This is a better question to think about as opposed to something like: What will this look like to everyone who hears about the result?

Resist the trappings of social media hype

I have seen a rise in subtle and not so subtle hyping up of children by coaches, trainers, and parents on the social media platforms. Being the 'family headline news' for some may be just the boost they need now and again, but be very careful. Without your being aware, you are taking the innocence of simple sports competition and turning it into a currency. This currency being **your self-esteem**. But children know when you are cashing in on their little bit of celebrity which you may be advertently or inadvertently helping to create. They can spot it in the way you tweet, the way you treat other parents, and the way you talk about lesser mortals (other families). A common tweet might be something along the lines of:

"Thanks to all who organized the tournament this weekend - A great event, lots of fun by all, and here is my Charlie with the trophy: #trophy"

There is a difference between pride and self-promotion; only you as a parent know your true intentions. If you are not careful, before you know it your child's sport results turn into a commodity for the coaches and the family brand. It starts to become 'big news' within the local community. If you sense there is an overemphasis on self-promotion, back off a little and keep the celebrations at home.

Build responsibility through choices

Who is mainly responsible for improvement, the performer, the coach, or you? Ultimately no matter how advanced a coach's or parent's support is, they cannot know the athlete's body and mind better than the athlete themselves. They must be the one who reflects and decides how they intend to make improvements for the next series of competitions. However, **telling someone to be responsible doesn't necessarily nurture responsibility.**

Making people aware of the **choices** they have and encouraging them to pick one of them to commit to and act upon, normally gives the person a sense of: *"Well I chose to do it like this, so it's my responsibility."* If you notice a commitment from them to improve their standards in the area they chose, then you can reward them for it. How you reward is up to you. But at least acknowledge you notice their efforts to make themselves better.

The Car Ride Home

This is the same approach as the car ride there! Swiftly move on from the experience. Pick out the positive parts*, **but only if the child wants to talk about it**.* Move the focus to other things. Let them be quiet if they want to. Talk it over if they want to. Do not dwell on the performance for too long, and again resist turning the car into an analysis suite. Leave that to the coach!! I recently spoke to a colleague working for the English Football (soccer) Association about this precise point. He has been responsible for nurturing many top international soccer players over the last fifteen years, but affirmed that if his own 14 year old child doesn't want to discuss aspects of his latest game during the car ride home, he will quickly move on to a discussion about the trivialities of life such as what they are having that evening for dinner, which movie he wishes to watch, or what schoolwork tasks he has to accomplish! There isn't a discussion of the game, as the *child doesn't want to talk about it!*

Be Eccentric – Who cares?

I have had to adapt myself constantly to effectively support my wife through all the different stages as her career has evolved to the top. My roles have included coach, psychologist, physical trainer, dietician, planner etc. My main role has simply entailed being her supportive, loving husband. My roles as a companion, listener, friend, chief supporter, and advisor has made us a strong pair, and it's assuming these widely diverse, and challenging roles that I am most proud of. From the outside I am often thought of as a madman, passionately intense one minute, yet totally relaxed the next. I am simultaneously liked and disliked. I'm thought of as an excellent buttress of support and as a heavy burden all in the same tournament! I'm sometimes perceived as being above my station, yet at other times as being too humble and too nice.

Often I am seemingly knowledgeable, but conversely at other times I'm seen as being completely clueless. 'Living through my wife' is a big insinuation that I've heard whispers of at times. The thing is all of these are true to some degree. It has not been a perfectly smooth ride, and, yes, my life has revolved around helping my wife's career move forward, particularly in the last five years. Yet the thing that has remained constant is that I am always prepared to believe I am capable of change and therefore improvement. I know I am valuable, and I know I have become a huge plus in our team. I will not be defined by other people's opinion of me. What is important is that I keep working on myself and who I believe I am. I have learned that when you think and behave like this, people don't know what box to put you in. They find it unsettling, particularly to those playing an acting role of themselves wherever they go. People like distinct boxes and labels for most things after all!

Last year, my mentor surprised me when he described me as a touch **'eccentric'**. I had never thought of myself that way before, to me eccentricity goes hand in hand with being strange and unpopular. I went to my phone typing in 'eccentric definition' and found the following: "A person of unconventional and slightly strange views or behavior." I immediately asked: "Slightly strange to whom? To everyone? Or just to those who don't agree with me?" At which my mentor said; "See what I mean!"

If being myself and trying new ideas without much care for what other people think is eccentric, then I urge you to be eccentric too. I did not set out to be eccentric and it was just a bit of a fun and a generalization after all, but there is a clear message there. If having eccentric behaviors means feeling free to change, adapt, and grow in the way you want, in a way that helps the people you love and respect, then go for it; it will free you up. You will enjoy seeing it in others too. You will notice their freedom to be themselves and have their own views independent of the conformists and judging order. The gossips, the followers, the institutionalized outlook, and the cardboard cut-out stereotypes are grounded in the herd mentality. It seems that many things in life are becoming increasingly uniform on a global scale. Whether this is by chance or design is another debate for another day. But I urge you to be a non-conformist, become your own best version of yourself, of course listen to popular opinion, but have the courage and confidence to evolve and be who you want to be even if that means you appear strange to some.

Laura Massaro: "Nothing is permanent unless you refuse to change!"

Here are some insightful perspectives from Laura:

"I put most of my success down to hard work. When I say hard work I don't mean training hard physically; my rivals can do that! Over my career my goal has been to surround myself with people who are trusted, extremely knowledgeable, and passionate. After I believe someone to have these characteristics, I give myself to them. I know that sounds a little odd, but once I fully believe in someone, I will do what they say to the letter. The English squash physical trainer once said to Danny, "Laura is easy to work with, if you told her to drink car oil, it will help you, then she would." Although when I was younger I never thought of that side of my personality as a strength, now I'm into my 12th year on tour I can see how those experiences have added up over the years. It's not just a case of I'm injured and I'll do as I'm told now in this moment because I have no other choice; it's having that attitude day in and day out!

I guess when I was younger it wasn't something I particularly thought of. To start with, it was underpinned by the fact that I always tried to respect people. I was brought up to have manners and face consequences if I didn't behave correctly. Getting told by my dad if I ever hit my racket on the wall I would never play squash again may seem a little harsh, but I can tell you that even to this day I have never broken a racket in anger. Not many professional players can say that! As my career moved on and I got older and matured, I started to see that there are two ways to train. Working hard is a must in both, but as I said earlier anyone with a bit of drive can do that. Added into the mix of work ethic and determination is staying completely open minded about everything. Over the last few years, it has become almost a mission of mine to finish my career leaving no stone unturned: Psychology, diet, physiology, technical aspects, physiotherapy, massage, yoga, hypnotherapy, books, and many more. If you lined up my team, all of whom have made a significant difference to my career, it would be a huge line and it's grown bigger over the last couple of years as I have looked for more stones to turn over!

David Pearson said to me when I won the prestigious British Open in 2013, "If I had to bet £10 when you were a youth player who would have won a British Open title from England, I would never have bet on you!" This might sound like it was a negative comment, but I couldn't have been happier. It is comments like that which make me beam with satisfaction. I know I'm on the right line with my mission to leave no stone unturned: Chasing, fighting, forcing me to push, to improve, and to be better every day.

Of course you never know if the next change will pay off; it's always a leap of faith trying something new. Trusting in the people around you helps, and there's a knowing in me that even if it doesn't work out that at least I know not to try it that way again! A few years ago I started working with a coach who wanted me to change my backhand. His backhand was great and as he was an ex-player from my local area who was respected, I trusted him fully. However, he wasn't a coach as such, and while trying to change my backhand I got it wrong. He never told me I wasn't doing it as he wanted, mainly because I don't think he knew how, but I was happy and I had something to work on.

My results were getting better, so when I turned up at the National Championships and heard a few whispers about my 'new swing', I didn't care; I just thought no one knew what I was trying to do. After parting ways (on good terms) with this particular coach my backhand ironed itself out and became better than ever. When I asked the ex-coach not so long ago what had happened, he just said: "Well, we needed to change it and your take on what I was asking you to do was what you did. It gave you a drive and something to work on so I left you to it." I replied: "But it wasn't right. Why didn't you tell me?" He laughed and said, "no one plays exactly the same way. It worked for you at the time and now you've moved on with your swing it's looking great!"

Looking back it's probably not the way I would have chosen to get to a better backhand, but by trusting him it didn't matter to me that it was slightly wrong. I improved at the time and with my open mindedness could change again when I needed to. Nothing is permanent, unless you refuse to change!"

As long as you're getting better!

No matter how small your change, if it helps then that is brilliant. Don't expect the huge difference too quick and notice the small gains.

In my example earlier the Canadian father I worked with recognized that his relationship with his son was better: "He laughed at my jokes again!" He wasn't bothered about his son's sports results at first; he saw the small gain. This encouraged him to enjoy these new behaviors because he felt he had cashed in. This is what makes it feel worthwhile to him. This is what makes him trust me and our work together.

And guess what? He can now see the improvements in his son more clearly. He sees his development as a young man and his growth in social skills, independence, and leadership. He feels more useful as a parent now, more pleased with his ability to help his son grow up and develop. Thus his fears were reduced and also all the negative feelings associated with inadequacy. **This alone improved his influence as a sports parent.** Just noticing small simple improvements in himself and in his son has unlocked huge joy and increased his commitment to keep sticking to new ideas and behaviors.

This is what this stage of the flight path is all about. It is about having the confidence and commitment to change what you do until they become easy habits. It is the only way you get better. Then if you can stay with it long enough, you will feel the benefits and notice your children reacting well to your improved leadership, and you will know it is worth the leap of faith. Your biggest prize is that you have built pride in yourself along with parenting skills you once imagined were out of reach.

Summary

Get busy implementing some new behaviors today. If you want different results, you must learn to act differently. You have not made changes if they only stay within your own mind.

Habits are hard to form at first but with continued effort they become ingrained and difficult to stop. Aim to improve on the three main phases of the competition experience: Before, during, and after.

Be flexible in your approaches. Avoid getting stuck. Be a touch eccentric, who cares if you come across as a little strange, as long as you are improving. Notice your improvements, this will give you the momentum to keep changing.

Notes & Reminders

Flight Path: Stage 7

'Let go, be there for Life'

Stage 7: Land Safely 'Let go, be there for Life'

The final stage of the flightpath for many parents is the part they find most emotionally challenging. It is the letting go, cutting the proverbial cord, and encouraging children to fly from the nest. You may still look out for them, still support them and love them as much as ever, but it is your time to step aside and pass over to them almost full responsibility for their sporting futures. Releasing people you love is simpler and certainly much less painful if your internal level of responsibility for that part of their life drops away. It is important that children feel this from you. If released skillfully and with strength, you communicate trust and confidence in their ability to go forward into the sporting world and fly solo.

'On Children'

Your children are not your children.
They are the sons and daughters of Life's longing for itself.
They come through you but not from you,
And though they are with you, yet they belong not to you.
You may give them your love but not your thoughts.
For they have their own thoughts.
You may house their bodies but not their souls,
For their souls dwell in the house of tomorrow,
which you cannot visit, not even in your dreams.
You may strive to be like them,
but seek not to make them like you.
For life goes not backward nor tarries with yesterday.
You are the bows from which your children
as living arrows are sent forth.
The archer sees the mark upon the path of the infinite,
and He bends you with His might
that His arrows may go swift and far.
Let your bending in the archer's hand be for gladness;
For even as He loves the arrow that flies,
so He loves also the bow that is stable.[87]

Kahlil Gibran

I asked our young professionals about their experiences of being 'let go' by their parents:

Me: Do you think parental influence needs to change depending on your age and experience?

Lauren Quigley: *Definitely. When I turned 17 I decided to move training environments to a bit of a tougher training setting and regime. I kind of recognized that my youth training environment wasn't mature enough and I knew I needed something to make me grow up. This was when my parents really left me alone a bit more. I think it was like, "You're old enough now go and sort it out yourself." I came home with a few complaints and issues, and they listened but told me to go and sort it out myself with the coach. Dad was particularly good with that. He encouraged me to sort my own problems out by talking and kind of standing up to my coach who can be sensitive. This has helped me so much because I had to confront my coaches and make a point to them. This has led to some good arguments that need to happen and it has toughened me up a lot.*

Me: So they gave you space and responsibility?

Lauren Quigley: *Yes, they didn't rescue me; so I stopped bringing them my moaning and small complaints. I was training with some adults too and I think their influence rubbed off on me. I used to worry and get a bit homesick for example; but as time went on I didn't want to worry my mother, so I stopped calling home. Naturally she wanted to just help me, but dad was good and explained I was just making things feel worse. My aunt was good too; she was also a professional swimmer. She said she'd wished she had enjoyed her trips away more when she swam, so I decided to look for the good stuff a bit more. I think that as I started to show more independence my parents backed off more because they worried less. Since then, I've really worked hard on reducing my worrying and I think it's helped us all.*

Me: You've contributed to calming them down then?

Lauren Quigley: *Yes, I think so. I broke the circle. I get the best out of them now because they trust me more I think. Plus I am 20 now so it's got even better as I've got older.*

There were times when mother was trying to impart too much help at the wrong time. I think because she could see where I was going wrong in some of my races, she used to criticize me or provide me with too much feedback after I had raced. As I got older, I just wanted my mother not an expert. When I race I only want to talk to my coach about it, because that's my coach's job. But I think my mother used to think it was her job as well. On the way to races she used to try and give me advice and tips and I just didn't want to talk about it because I get nervous and it makes it worse. I just wanted to think about other things which could cause arguments and more stress. It's hard because she really wanted to help, but I had to work it out for myself.

Adam Henley: *Luckily for me my parents took a step back as they know me really well. They know I won't be pushed as a person. I always took it one step at a time just thinking of the next year. I am quite deep and self-aware. My parents knew pushing me would be the worst thing; it would have closed me off. They knew how to treat me. I think this was massive in helping me deal with all the highs and lows. It kept me balanced even though sometimes I did get a bit closed off; but overall at least I wasn't getting too hyped up. I do think it really helps if your natural personality is strong and you can almost push pressure away when you are young. You definitely need that skill when you grow up.*

Me: Did parental support change depending on your age?

Adam Henley: *Yes, a little. As soon as I signed the professional contract I moved out of home and took on lots more personal responsibility. I was going to be operating in a man's world. The dynamics of my lifestyle changed and I felt more independent. My mother was great with this and she demonstrated **trust** by letting me go and never sulking about it. I can live by myself and I am very proud of that. We speak quite a bit, but there's been a shift in my independence and this has been important.*

Scott Fitzgerald: *My parents have never been controlling really, so nothing much has changed. I've seen other kids' parents be in their son's faces a lot which luckily I've never had. My mother was the stricter parent and actually didn't want me to be a boxer. At first we had to keep it from her in case she got too stressed and asked me to stop. My parents separated when I was younger, so they have had different ways of bringing me up. They had a good mix, with my dad being more of a friend and advisor and my mother being a little stricter; always emphasizing the importance of school and giving me more discipline.*

My mother is great because in the end she always let me make my own decisions, it is just that she would worry more and sometimes see the negatives in things. As soon as she realized I had decided that I was going to be a boxer and fight she became my biggest fan.

I think because they have been firm but fair with me that I have never had pressure put on me or felt they were interfering in my life too much. I have the desire to achieve because I want to do it not because they made me feel guilty about it. I really feel like my own man, and I think this was big in helping me win my Gold medal last year.

"Parents can only give advice on the right paths, but the final forming of a person's character lies in their own hands."[88]

Anne Frank

The help illusion

During my many years of teaching and coaching thousands of young people, I have noticed certain patterns in those who go on to be successful and happy. Below are some of my observations and conclusions; I try to explain how less can lead to more when it comes to nurturing young people. Here is my take on something I have called 'The Help Illusion' and how I believe it has crept in to modern sports in greater force.

Who makes you better? "I do!"

It may sound simple to say, but in my experiences those youngsters who thrive clearly have a wisdom that 'they are in control of their own improvement'. I think above everything else, this is the discerning factor in their success. If you asked them, *"Who makes you better?"* many would instantly respond, "Me! I make myself better." They have a sense of personal control and self-confidence which allows them to take this responsibility on their young shoulders. The key word is **independence**, and it leads to fantastic results in their psychology and their behaviors. They seek out the appropriate people for advice, they bounce back from failures, they risk, they dream, and they improve themselves at fast rates in many areas of their lives. **This develops character.** In sports, they win. They win big in fact. They become great role models, they are a joy to work with, and in the end they always improve. They inspire others around them and they make their coaches and parents look better than they are!

The opposite of this are those people who generally look to others to improve them. They hand over responsibility to teachers, coaches, parents, trainers, physiotherapists, psychologists etc. They tend to assume that if they listen to the expertise and take the incoming motivation, then they will progress as if touched by a magic wand. Yet because of this flawed belief, improvement is rare and blame becomes common. Without the inner belief that they have the independence and gumption to stick to incoming advice and support, improvements are rare, and at the very best they are temporary. Yo-yo cycles of enthusiasm do nothing for long lasting change and it is with inevitable sadness that such people eventually fail. Nothing is seen through and little is earned. Ultimately, fear creeps in to those spaces that were supposed to be full with self-esteem, and so we look for credible excuses to ease the pain. Credible excuses in sport are readily available under categories of: Injuries, Bad Luck, Poor Officiating, Cultural Problems, Ineffective Coaching, Other Lifestyle Demands, Inappropriate Equipment, and Lack of Support.

Parental reflections

Looking back on your life, have there been times when you have searched for the magic wand to fix your problems? And if so, what were the lasting outcomes? E.g. a popular diet, a gizmo that will make you fit, a coach or book that promised success?

Which particular episodes of your life earned you your personal confidence and self-esteem when growing up?

In his book <u>How Children Succeed</u>,[89] Paul Tough explains that in the lowest echelons of society where deprivation of basics in opportunity and support exist, children do not stand a chance of success; so there is a minimum level of help required. Yet the same struggle can be said of those children who raised in cosseted settings are bailed out of predicaments by helicopter parents and never allowed to fail or overcome adversity on their own initiative. I see this very much in transition phases from the youth to the professional game in sports. Unless blessed with exceptional ability, most youngsters who want to compete internationally or professionally will hit big barriers. They will be rocked back by realizations of the struggle ahead in their sports, just at the same time they are understanding the basic challenges of becoming responsible, self-sufficient adults and all that role entails. Without the background of overcoming challenges and facing failures, many youngsters just fall away bewildered and depressed. As the saying goes: **"A kid who is born on third base and grows up thinking they hit a triple is not going to survive against the kid who actually hit a triple to get to third base"**.

> *"The best teachers are those who show you where to look but don't tell you what to see."*[90]
>
> *Alexandra Trenfor*

The help industry

The 'help industry' (of which I am part of), comprised of coaches, analysts, physiotherapists, psychologists, nutritionists, strength and conditioning trainers, performance directors, private tutors, therapists etc. has clearly been vital for professional performers in sports and business. Expertise is provided to already successful athletes; something that has clearly been a positive move at world level sport. This has been epitomized very well by the U.K's British Cycling team, led by Sir David Brailsford. Their 'marginal gains' philosophy (which breaks down every factor behind riding a bike, and then tries to improve upon every single one of these factors by 1%) has attracted significant media attention and hype in recent times; particularly in the U.K.[91] They have certainly achieved fantastic success, and nobody can dispute that.

But, the absolutely imperative point for discussion here is that **great performers make the helpers look good**. There are many 'so called' gurus of coaching and training, who have helped many world class performers. The 'marginal gains' philosophy, for instance, has supported these top cyclists in their efforts, in which they have accrued wonderful success. But we must always remember a crucial point: It's simply the icing on a very well baked cake; a cake that has already been baked by the performers! Conversely, many widely heralded coaching gurus have had either limited impact or negative impact with many other athletes. In fact, when you pry behind the headlines of many a 'super-coach', the ratios of success more often than not are negative.

There is a term for this phenomenon, the 'Halo Effect.' It is the presumption that this special person, or group of people, or school system or whatever, can fix all your problems for you, and by some special power make it almost guaranteed. We scratch around for these magic people in a hope that their magic will rub off on us as it has for **all** their previous disciples. Believe me, I have been there and actually been convinced myself. There was a time I was foolish enough to think I could help anyone improve, as long as they invested in my secrets and my beliefs. I have followed mentors and heroes of mine believing they had all the answers I was searching for.

I used to think, "If only I knew what they knew, if I could be who they are and do what they do, then maybe I could also reach the **Promised Land**!" Well in my experience, there is no such place, no fool-proof method to coaching, and certainly not one magic method being effective for everyone on earth!

No Promised Land - Parent reflection

Have you felt this way about being a parent? Living as if there exists a standard of parenting that you just can't attain yet?

Why did you read this book? Was it to find a magic trick that would instantly solve all your sports parenting ordeals and stresses? Or was it to add one or two bits of wisdom to your unfolding, complicated, and organic life as a parent who has children who compete?

Having almost completed the book, how happy or disappointed are you about the quantity of effort and skill I have encouraged you to invest?

If you are disappointed, then I feel you have fallen prey to the **'help illusion'**. A basic con trick where you have been duped into a belief that somebody out there by information alone can do your work for you.

What has become ever more noticeable is that the 'Halo effect' goes further than just making the individual helper look like an 'improvement God', but actually starts to make the whole help industry look necessary to young people and their loving parents. As we see more evidence of professional role models incorporating increasing amounts of support and expertise into their preparations, there is a tendency that we all need to do it, and you bet there are plenty of people ready to step in and fill the market. Many universities and training organisations churn out thousands of people all ready and raring to fill those roles, and they are all willing to be paid handsomely for their services. They make careers out of helping, providing expertise, and supporting in any way a youngster can request. It is certainly big business!

Even equipment and technology have gotten in on the act of the 'help illusion'. 'All the gear and no idea' has become a popular joke for those who look the part yet struggle with playing the part! Although it's a bit of fun, there is actually a key point there. Responsibility gets passed to uniforms, equipment, footwear, facilities, and machinery or dietary supplements to make the job easier for you. Not forgetting all the latest recovery clothing, sports drinks, and self-massage tools. Of course, all these things can be helpful (as my wife attested earlier in this book) and some basic standard of support needs to exist, but the moment you believe it is the things outside of you that improve you then you have fallen once more for the 'help illusion'.

Precarious times

Many individuals involved in supporting athletes have wonderful ideas and expertise, but what can happen is that the more they help you, the less personal responsibility you feel to move yourself forwards. Parents all over the world can tend to forget this point when considering their child's coaching support. Many parents believe their child **must be** coached by a highly qualified or college level coach in order to guarantee their game will be taken to the 'next level'! They are consistently bombarded with promises, and sold on the idea that their child's progression in the sport lies solely in the hands of the 'expert' who is coaching them. This is a notion that goes completely unchallenged the vast majority of the time. But on a deeper level, being hypnotized into believing other people are responsible for our success means we do not earn pride or pure self-confidence, and the cycle perpetuates. Self-sufficiency becomes a rare commodity in our young people. **Youngsters begin to think that because they are characters, they have character!** Get the balance right between seeking the support you need while being self-reliant. Do not feel that you have to join in and disseminate this emerging culture.

Don't deprive them of the struggle

What is never going to change is that we have to overcome struggle in order to strengthen ourselves. Just like the principle of progressive overload when lifting heavier weights to gain more muscle mass, things must be hard for us; so we go inside and change. Pain is a massive personal motivator. We will do anything to avoid embarrassment or letting somebody down who we respect. Being banned, losing, or being outplayed are all powerful energies that can be used to your advantage in the long term if you let them sting you. **And let them sting you must.** Top performers always say how they learn a lot more from the bad times, as opposed to the good times. That not only takes a certain mindset, but a certain amount of **suffering** must also be experienced. It is the suffering that can be your ultimate character builder. Wanting to avoid that feeling again, and wanting to replace it with success really drives people on to great things. People don't run out of car fuel very often do they? Somehow they always get to the pumps! Even those 'forgetful' types! Why I wonder – the prospect of too much suffering perhaps?

Bottom line: Look for a struggle, embrace it, and overcome it. If you let youngsters feel it before you soften it by making excuses, they will earn genuine personal strength when they come through it. Support them mildly, but use struggle as a character building tool. Take an example from former Manchester United Head Coach Sir Alex Ferguson who knew exactly how to harness the pain of defeat to move his players on to English Premier League domination: ***"Every time we finished second, which happened five times, we won it the following season. There's some merit in getting defeated – even though I'd never want to make it a habit."*** [92]

BE CAREFUL

Do not feel that you must add to the suffering too much. The competitive loss or poor performance should hurt anyway. In my experience, if it does not hurt and they seem full of apathy, then you will only be 'putting the cart before the horse' anyway by trying to make it hurt for them! There is nothing wrong with being honest, but avoid adding guilt or blame or punishment; simply get out of the way and let the persons feel it themselves.

This will be very hard for you if you are used to rescuing or you are worrying about your own reputation as a parent. We all have our ways of getting attention after all, and helping when other 'nasty people' won't help out is a guaranteed way of earning such attention! Resist giving the solutions, resist diverting or softening of the experience, and give the situation space. Allow the contemplation and then ask them how they intend to move on. By all means stay supportive and humane, but let the reality of the hurt stay a little. It will not kill them off, but it will more likely reveal the truth about how much **they** really want to commit to avoiding this in future.

Hard times create hard people, cosy times less so.

"Over the years I became better at judging the influence of background on a British player, because we would know the family backgrounds and the schools they attended. Until around the mid 1990's the youngsters would understand their place in the pecking order at the club. They would be responsible for removing mud from boots, cleaning the dressing room, and doing 'balls and bibs' [making sure all the practice equipment was ready to go]. Those sorts of rituals probably just made them yearn for success even more."[93]

Sir Alex Ferguson

In terms of character development and personal drive, youngsters of today have had it harder in many ways. This is because as many of them have aged, they have so many people immediately offering to take misery away from them. They have been inadvertently spoiled because there are more offerings of a bright future. It happens at school, at least in the UK. There doesn't appear to be a way to **fail** anymore. When people fail they fall back to a certain level of luxury, care, and attention. A re-sit of a **'final'** exam paper, or a bit of easy coursework will always allow people to progress without too much trouble, pain, or stress.

Even from the earliest schooldays, (especially in the western world) youngsters are shielded from the stark realities of life. As many of us can attest from our own experiences, children are constantly told to delete out any schoolwork mistakes with an eraser. They aren't allowed to have any remnant of a mistake – it's a culture of complete denial and shame about error! Mistakes are discouraged and frowned upon; they are not utilized as the fantastic learning opportunities that they should be, or used as moments in which children can be shown they won't get everything correct first time. From the earliest ages it seems youngsters are wrapped in cotton wool, and protected from the ways of how it will be in the 'big wide world'. But, unfortunately, as many of us can also attest, that's just not the way life is!

But it is not the case that all people must come from tough backgrounds in order to 'make it' as a professional. However, there is a certain quality in those that fight their way out of tough situations. There is a particular intelligence forged by experience, and a desire to escape and rise up. In some cases it`s almost like they are desperate to escape and prove people wrong, as we discussed in earlier in the book. For instance, we witness this so often with many South American soccer players. As youngsters, top performers such as Luis Suárez of FC Barcelona, Sergio

Agüero of Manchester City FC, ex-Manchester United FC forward Carlos Tevez, and countless Brazilian soccer players all came from abject poverty and deprivation. It is probably no coincidence that many of them have similar playing styles too. This style is based on an insatiable hunger to never give in, a fantastic work-rate, and a kind of blasé attitude towards the opponent they are facing. It's like they have an outlook based on the notion: **"Bring it on, I came from utter adversity to be where I am today; nothing will stop me!"**

This is not to say you have to have a 'tough life' to become this way. Many champions have come from luxurious surroundings where life has been easier. Challenge and adversity can come at different depths for different people. One person's Everest is another person's walk in the park. So the message is: Find ways to set appropriate challenges for your young competitors; both in the performance arena and in life too. Refrain from making excuses for them, reinforce your agreed ground rules through consistent discipline, and allow some suffering to remain before molly coddling and rescuing the situation. Yes you can empathize, and in certain cases sympathize, but remember the saying I quoted in the Introduction: **"Smooth seas do not make skilful sailors."**[94]

Bottom Line: **Youngsters need 'wake up' calls along their pathway.** There have to be times where there is no 'side door' to take and a level of fear that you may never escape this problem if you don't do something about it. This is much harder to experience if there is always somebody to sponsor you, pay for you, or act as a constant 'get out of jail for free' card. Reality must bite hard on occasion. Deep self-reflection must be more valued than those 'motivating talks' with the support team. Parents must have the strength to let their young sports players go through tough times which feel relevant to them. If this be through discipline, loss, temporary withdrawal, agreed consequences, or enforced rules and boundaries, then so be it. They have to tackle head-on the challenges and pain at some point.

Roger Federer's take

In an interview with House of Commons (U.K Parliament) speaker John Bercow, Roger Federer supported the view that young players need space from their parents, while understanding they have a responsibility to perform and give it their all:

"Parental support and advice is very important to make you understand it's a privilege to be able to go to tennis lessons and play tournaments. So the least a kid can do is give it their best effort and best attitude. At the same time, the parents also need to give space to

the kid and the coaches so they can work and travel by themselves – the parents don't always need to babysit them through their entire career. That's why today when my parents tell me: "You know what, we want to come to every single tournament you play on the tour," I would say, yes please, and come see me. I don't mind spending every day with you guys for the year.

But if they tell me, "we don't want to come see you play because we really don't enjoy it", that's cool too. And that's what I hope every parent can look forward to with their kid.

It needs to be both ways and for me that worked very well – I got the space, but I also felt the pressure, the need to perform."[95]

More recognition, less attention

Something that can really help parents create **space** that Roger Federer talks about is being able to distinguish between attention and recognition. If you think about it, what we really strive for from our loved ones is recognition. We want them to say, "Well done, good job. You did really well at that. You should be proud of yourself." We want to be recognized for our efforts, our special talents, and how we contribute. In particular, we want to be recognized by our leaders, and nobody more so than our parents. Of course, we want to have some level of attention and interest in us, but very quickly this alone can amount to interference.

Attention without recognition = interference!

Parent reflection

Think about your own parents: Did you want their attention or recognition more? To this very day, you probably want them to say, "You did well in life. You are very special and I am very proud of what you have accomplished and who you have become." This is recognition. It doesn't take much does it? Yet the power of it is extraordinary. It fills us with greater belief and an energy to take on new challenges and risks. The biggest tick in the box we could ever get!

Our parents are perhaps the most powerful people in our lives and influence us continuously, even after they have passed on. Arguably we live as if one day we will eventually sit down with them both in a formal situation and ask: "Ok guys, how did I do? Are you proud of me? Did I do life well?" No matter how old we get, we can rapidly regress in the role of a sensitive child when around our parents, particularly when we feel they are interfering in our decisions: "I don't need your help you know, I can do that without your help. Can you not see how independent I've become? I am grown up you know! Wow, you are so out of touch!"

It's not like we go about our lives consciously trying to impress our parents or conform to their notion of a good life, but deep down we crave their recognition and approval. We do this with many others in life too, but our parents usually hold most sway. Ironically, this can become annoying and can cause great tension and trepidation within the relationship, and if not doused down can become awfully painful and hostile. I can see this so clearly when I observe children and their parents at sporting competitions. Teenage years are particularly difficult as youngsters crave independence yet still yearn for their parents' approval. It confuses them, so often they just lash out at any form of criticism, fussing, or perceived lack of interest. I am sure you have felt this force on one occasion or another.

Only at funerals, or through suffering life-threatening illness in later life, do we seem to wake up to how simple it was to just love each other. For a while the game stops and we feel free of judgement, hostility, and blame. You are the same flesh and blood, and that is all that matters. Not approval, not success, not relief, just love and acceptance!

We do not need to play this waiting game. All we need to do is recognize each other more often. Have nice conversations, find a way to enjoy your time with your parents, and know as you live that love and acceptance is all the support you'll ever need. There will be ups and downs of course, but always go back to love and freedom. It really is that simple.

Notice the good stuff - it is there

You can give recognition for simple things. You can say something like: "Hey, I know I haven't been able to see you play a lot recently, and I know you are not getting the results you want yet but I have noticed how determined you have been. I appreciate that, and the fact that you have done it by yourself a bit more lately shows me you have what it takes to get better. Well done. Is there anything I can help you with or have you got it covered?"

Let's say you attend a performance and support your son. He wins, but in your opinion plays below standard and in some ways was a little lucky. What would be your normal reaction if he comes over to you and asks: "What did you think?"

(A) *An honest and direct critical appraisal of how he must improve next time, or else?*

(B) *A giddy celebration just praising the win and affirming how marvelous the entire team had performed, frightened to say the wrong thing.*

(C) *A softened simple critique praising the ability to find a way to win followed by the question, "What are your thoughts?"*

Option (C) is the most balanced response so I urge you to remain this way. By asking their opinion while offering some light interpretations of their performance, you are giving **recognition** to their efforts, and your trust in them to come up with a valid critique themselves. You are interested in them. You are recognizing their independence while adding a few requested thoughts of your own.

Option (A) and Option (B) although different are too much about the parent and generally too involved. They are hyping up the importance of a win and the building importance of avoiding a future loss. It is **attention** not recognition. This is not letting go. It is holding on. This is clinging to your control and sense of responsibility for their sporting futures. You may not actually come out and say it, but this is what you communicate: "It is very important that you please me because you reflect my parenting and my state of happiness, and ultimately that affects how much I love you."

If you think this is incorrect, think about why you get so edgy even to this day when your own parents try to tell you what to do!

Advice from an astronaut: 'Aim to be a ZERO'

One of the major things that helped me be a better leader for my wife was to stop trying to be a hero all the time. I had to learn to be a zero!

I was beginning to come to this realization myself through experiences of trying too hard to help her. I wanted to be the superstar husband and coach that could help Laura make all her dreams come true. Lots of my identity was wrapped up in my wife's success, and I wanted to make sure I made my impact. **This was a big mistake.** Although this is hard to admit, this was evident by the fact that on many occasions my effect was negative. Enter the Astronaut! Canadian Astronaut Chris Hadfield is perhaps the most famous spaceman in the world at the moment, and through his YouTube music videos and incredible photographs from space he has brought 'Outer Space' closer to the masses. In his excellent book <u>An Astronaut's Guide to Life on Earth</u>, he transmitted a very powerful and simple revelation that has helped me tremendously. Here it is:

"Over the years, I've realized that in any new situation, whether it involves an elevator or a rocket ship, you will almost certainly be viewed in one of three ways. As a minus one: actively harmful, someone who creates problems. Or as a zero: Your impact is neutral and doesn't tip the balance either one way or the other. Or you'll be seen as a plus one: Somebody who actively adds value. Everyone wants to be a plus one, of course. But proclaiming your plus-oneness at the outset almost guarantees you'll be perceived as a minus one, regardless of the skills you bring to the table or how you actually perform. This might seem self-evident, but it can't be, because so many people do it."[96]

Not only did this sum up my personal past experiences, but it correlated directly with what I see parents struggling with when they enter the new environments of competitive youth sport. I have always maintained that I believe 99% of parents have positive intentions for their children, yet through over-eagerness and a desire to help, they often end up having the opposite effect. This is the very root of the problem and so obviously explained. **Sports parents everywhere are trying to be Plus Ones instead of being confident to be a Zero, which will ultimately have a Plus One effect. This is what grandparents do so well, and why they often provide excellent support for youngsters.**

Hadfield continues to explain:

"A zero isn't a bad thing to be. You're competent enough not to create problems. Tom Marshburn (fellow crewmate) never imposed his expertise on anyone or told us what to do. Instead, he was competent and helpful. If I needed him, he was there in an instant but he never elbowed me out of the way to demonstrate his superior skills or made me feel small for not knowing how to do something. Everyone on our team knew that Tom was a plus one. He didn't have to tell us."[97]

The best parents I have met and observed are just like Tom. The best teachers are, and the best coaches are too. There is a calmness, a certainty, and a powerful confidence all coming from their humility and wisdom to be steady. They don't crave savior or hero status. They may all have different personality styles and various skillsets, but they understand the simplicity and net benefits of being the zero.

Hadfield concluded:

"If you are confident in your abilities and sense of self, it's not nearly as important to you whether you're steering the ship or pulling the oar. Your ego isn't threatened. You believe everything you're doing contributes to the mission in some way. Still, I am human. I like recognition and I like feeling that others consider me a plus one. Which is why, as we approached the International Space Station on December 21, 2012, I consciously reminded myself to aim to be a zero once we got inside. Two decades into my career as an astronaut I felt as close to a plus one as I ever had."[98]

Fortunately, in respect to my personal situation, I have calmed down and found ways to act more as a zero despite my strong natural urges to be recognized. It has taken work, and like Chris Hadfield, I have to consciously remind myself to stay steady; particularly at sports competitions. I have improved my ability to just listen more than I used to, and I resist the temptation to constantly jump in to rescue situations. I wait more to be asked questions without professing my views. This has benefitted me as much as anything I have ever learned in my life. It helps me the most in pressure situations at tournaments, and I know from talking with my wife and with those I coach that they feel far more loved and empowered. My enthusiasm remains steadfast, but the panic and over complication of things has diminished considerably. They have thrived off my trust in them, and to my surprise it has been a remarkably easier way to live. Aiming to be the zero, who would have thought it could be so easy!

Consider it a rite of passage

Most societies have some sort of 'rite of passage' ceremony to represent children becoming adults. In the West, it may be graduation ceremonies, passing their driving exam, an 18th or 21st birthday, getting married, leaving home, getting a first full-time job, buying your first house, or even becoming a parent. These are all key moments where a youngster has crossed some type of threshold in their lives. These are all ideal times for you to have a conversation and let go of more responsibility each time. They are occasions where you can recognize their growth and raise your expectations of them in terms of independence and responsibility. Thinking of these life events as 'rites of passage' will help remind you that you are suddenly dealing with young adults as opposed to children. They will benefit from your acknowledgement of this and your confidence to let them fly the family nest. After all, they can always come home and get the boosts they will certainly need.

In the brilliant movie 'The Shawshank Redemption', the character 'Red' affirms:

"I have to remind myself that some birds aren't meant to be caged. Their feathers are just too bright. And when they fly away, the part of you that knows it was a sin to lock them up does rejoice."[99]

Final comment

Recently, due to writing this book, I have thanked both my parents for giving me the space to grow and learn for myself; particularly when I was in my late teens. My mother gave birth to me aged 17 herself, so maybe it was no big deal to them.

I told my parents recently: "You gave me the gifts of freedom and responsibility - Did you know what you were doing?" My Dad explained simply: "Well we didn't abandon you, did we? You knew we were there if you needed us. We just got out of the way and left you to it."

Easy as that then – typical! It has taken me a whole chapter to say that!

Summary

Encourage independence and beware of the 'Help Illusion' created by the ever-growing 'Help Industry'.

Recognition is more required than attention. So notice the good stuff more often, and leave them alone a little more than usual.

Struggle is important: Don't deprive them of that gift by continuing to rescue and excuse. Aim to be a Zero in order to have a Plus One effect. You won't have to tell them you're a Plus; they'll feel it.

Consider your letting go as an important 'rite of passage' all youngsters deserve.

Notes & Reminders

Final words

I asked some of the individuals who contributed to this book to offer their final piece of wisdom based on their experiences in competitive youth and senior sport. Here they are:

David Pearson

I would say that it is so important to remember the person behind the performer. At the end of the day, if your children know you love them unconditionally, they will always be far more likely to succeed in whatever they choose to do. After this, then talk to them as players, but do it at the right time and in the right setting. Real happiness lies in love and strong relationships, not in attaining medals and titles.

Think of the long process or the journey more than just now. I am talking beyond sport too. Are they developing into well-rounded people who can cope in the wide world? You want mentally healthy people who will be stable, who can hold relationships together, and be a positive member of society. It isn't always about the winning; although that is good to strive for. However, winning is no good if the athlete turns out to be a nasty, frustrated, or mentally and emotionally fragile person.

I have witnessed many so called 'winners' in sport who have been champions as youth players and seniors who have struggled with normal life. For some reason, while they and everyone around them were pursuing victory after victory, everyone forgot what life away from sport was all about. I think parents can really help prevent this by not getting wrapped up in the 'bubble' of sport and by simply reminding their children that other things in life are more important.

Along similar lines I would say it is important to know when to 'back off' and when to 'pick your battles' with youngsters. Getting your timing right is vital, and often it's not what you say but how you say it; what tone of voice you use, and what facial expression you have. Where you decide to make a point is important too. Do it in a place where they feel comfortable. Certainly, don't approach them in public or in the car where they can feel trapped.

Overall, there is no set remedy or one way to parent. It's like this with coaching; it is not a complete science. You try your best and sometimes *you're dammed if you do and dammed if you don't; but one must never give up learning. I know this as a father **and** as a coach.*

Lauren Quigley

*Overall, I would say that it is really important not to **smother** your child; let them grow. Give them space to go with their coaches. You have to **trust** the coach and then the **coach** must trust the parents. So find a good coach whom you trust, and let them do the coaching! It's about finding that balance, and knowing how and when to step in. Everyone is different, so you've got to know what gets the best reaction. Most important is that you all want what is best and you move on after arguments. You're all going to be right and wrong at different times, but if you know you share the same vision and you are aligned with what's important in the big picture, then it will work.*

In my experiences with swimming, I have noticed that all the best parents are calm and strong people. They are confident, but not too arrogant, and they do well in their own lives away from their kids, such as in business or in other sports. They are grounded, and it keeps the kids grounded too. My parents are definitely like that as well, and for me overall it's probably been the biggest factor behind my progression and growth as an athlete.

Adam Henley

I'd say: "Go and tell your kids to practice technique and skills much more. It's a lot easier when you're younger to acquire skills and good technique. In relation to soccer, I would always encourage young kids to work on both feet when they practice, and they should constantly sample different positions. I would always emphasise the aspects of fun and enjoyment. When you compete at the professional level you realize how vital it is to be more technically proficient, as opposed to being tactically astute. It's much harder to pick up quality technique when you're older, so you must do it when you are young; you can't miss 'windows of opportunity' during the early years".

I would tell parents to always focus on keeping calm. They should always emphasize the enjoyment aspect of the sport. If they look bored or stressed, invite them to take a good break and do something else for a bit. Everything can't be all about being better at sports. My message to the parents is: Let the coaches' coach, and you keep your perspective by encouraging schoolwork and by supporting your children with everything they do at home. A young player will always improve just because they are young and growing. So sometimes just leave them alone having fun; and if it's meant to be for them, it's meant to be!

My parents were brilliant throughout my development. Even when I became professional they didn't get carried away. They were really honest with me and didn't let me get carried away either.

I went through a period where I picked up a few injuries in a short space of time. This kept me out of the team for a while but my parents were still positive and didn't get too down. They just explained that this was the start of another long journey for me, like the one I had taken from 7 to 18 years old in the Academy system where I displayed resilience and a long-term perspective. I really needed this 'big picture' type of honesty again during the time I suffered those injuries, because I was starting to doubt myself. They told me what I needed to hear, not what I wanted to hear! They said, "There is a lot of hard work ahead and it's like starting again Adam. You need to show the same attitude you displayed when you were a young kid." These kinds of messages, along with the same ones from my coaches, really helped me get back on track. It's that level of understanding and honesty, not pressure, through all the ups and downs that makes the difference when you are an aspiring young athlete.

Scott Fitzgerald

I would say it is really important that you don't get carried away if your child shows some promise. They need to 'want it' themselves, and not be looking to achieve just to please their parents. Parents give up a lot of time and effort, but the child shouldn't feel guilty about that. If they feel like stopping or slowing down, then that is up to them.

I don't think everyone can be a champion junior boxer; some have just got the talent, courage, and physique when they're younger. It's not fair that some parents expect their kids to be champions; not everyone can get to this level. They can enjoy boxing, and they should try their best at all times, but being a top-level champion is a special and unique achievement that only a few ever experience. I feel that sometimes parents need to remember this premise. Maybe they box for different reasons, like learning about discipline, humility, or fitness. Or kids might box simply because they love the social part of it. This is probably the case in lots of sports.

John Trower

Lead them strongly, and let them know where they are in the pecking order. They should know they are loved, but not smothered. Sport is a mixture of play, fun, and structure; as is life. Set them boundaries, and make sure they realize they 'know their place'. If they never know how to stay grounded, they will never learn to deal with adversity and challenge in later life. Sport will put you 'under the line' often enough, and you have to be able to handle that and work through it. It cannot just be given to you. Your competitors will not do that; life will not do that.

*If you are a parent of a child with a **high level of sporting potential** and they have success early on, be careful not to be too egotistical about it. Keep calm about it, because if you don't, you will change your child's motivational climate to one consumed by too much ego. Express your congratulations to them, but refrain from becoming too high and overdoing the adulation! This will be the same for unexpected losses: Avoid going too low and depressed about things. Show them that your emotions are in control whether they have won or lost. In the end this brings stability to them. Above all, be strong and remember that you are the adult, they are the child.*

Me!

*The last thing I would like to say is 'do your best.' If at the end of your life, you can be proud of your efforts to raise young adults you believe in, then what more can you do? **Use Competitive sport as one of the vehicles to do this.** Use the 'Winning Flightpath' I have proposed, and give it a chance by sticking to it. Fit it into your family philosophy and circumstances so it becomes **your** version that works for you.*

Perfection in parenting is a myth. Perfection in sport is a myth too. It is all just chaos and very hard to deal with at times. I have learned that those parents who recognize this are the most open to change and improvement, because as parents they acknowledge many of their own shortcomings and accept that real life is unpredictable, yet at the same time rewarding. Being this way usually means they will hold less fear and exude more strength. Where others tend to panic, they see the funny side and move on. Where others dominate and control, they support and enforce agreed boundaries.

Where others just see an athlete, they see a young person.

Where others only see the sports competition, they see life as a whole.

Where others lose in the short-term and the long-term, they are **'Winning Parents'** *forever.*

Good luck!

References

1. Gore, M. L. (1993) *Walking in my shoes* (Recorded by Depeche Mode) On Songs of Faith and Devotion (CD). London: Mute Records.

2. Côté, J. (1999) The influence of family in the development of talent in sport. *The Sport Psychologist*, 13, 395-417.

3. Zamperini, L. and Rensin, D. (2014) *Don`t give up, don`t give In: Lessons from an extraordinary life*, p.21. New York: Dey Street Books.

4. Côté, J. (1999) The influence of family in the development of talent in sport. *The Sport Psychologist*, 13, 395-417.

5. Shedd, J. In: Shapiro, F. R. (2006) *The Yale book of quotations*, p.705. Portland, Maine: The Mosher Press.

6. African Proverb. In: Brady, A. (2011) *When all else fails...stAND*, p.69. Maitland, Florida: Xulon Press.

7. Lee, H. In: Manser, M.H. (2001) *The Westminster collection of Christian quotations*, p.309. Louisville: Westminster John Knox Press.

8. Robinson, K. (2006) *Do schools kill creativity?* TED Talk, accessed online at: https://www.ted.com/talks/ken_robinson_says_schools_kill_creativity/transcript?language=en

9. Wooden, J. In: Nater, S., and Gallimore, R. (2006) *You haven't taught until they have learned – John Wooden's teaching principles and practices*. Morgantown, W.V: Fitness Information Technology.

10. Robbins, T. (2002) *Lessons in mastery*. Simon & Schuster Audio/Nightingale-Conant; Abridged edition.

11. Robinson, K. (2006) *Do Schools Kill Creativity?* TED Talk, accessed online at: https://www.ted.com/talks/ken_robinson_says_schools_kill_creativity/transcript?language=en

12. Wooden, J. (1997) *Wooden: A lifetime of observations and reflections on and off the court*. New York: McGraw-Hill Books.

13. Nardi, D. (2011) *Neuroscience of personality: Brain savvy insights for all types of people.* Los Angeles, CA: Radiance House.

14. Cain, S. (2013) *Quiet: The Power of introverts in a world that can't stop talking.* London: Penguin Books.

15. Bayne, R. (1995) *The Myers-Briggs type indicator: A critical review and practical guide.* Cheltenham: Nelson Thomas Ltd.

16. Riso, D. R., and Hudson, R. (1999) *The wisdom of the enneagram: Complete guide to psychological and spiritual growth for the nine personality types.* New York: Bantam Press.

17. The Naranjo Institute (2011) *The Enneagram.* The Naranjo Institute, accessed online at: http://www.naranjoinstitute.org.uk/enneagram.html

18. Epstein, D. (2014) *The sports gene.* London: Yellow Jersey Press.

19. Ericsson, K.A., and Charness, N. (1994) Expert performance its structure and acquisition. *American Psychologist*, 49(8), 725-747.

20. Epstein, D. (2014) *The sports gene.* London: Yellow Jersey Press.

21. Ibid

22. Craig, I. In: Witts, J. (2015) *The gene genie.* Runner's World Magazine, pp.50-55, Plattsburgh, NY: Hearst Rodale Ltd.

23. Hellstedt, J.C. (1987) The coach/parent/athlete relationship. *The Sports Psychologist* 1, 151-160.

24. Wuerth, S., Lee, M. S., and Alferman, D. (2004) Parental involvement and athletes' career in youth sport. *Psychology of Sport and Exercise, 5,* 21-33.

25. Chelladurai, P (1990) Leadership in sports: A review. *International Journal of Sport Psychology.* 21(4), 328-354.

26. Ibid

27. MacNamara, Á., Button, A., and Collins, D. (2010) The role of psychological characteristics in facilitating the pathway to elite performance. Part 1: identifying mental skills and behaviours. *The Sport Psychologist.* 24, 52-73.

28. Goleman, D. (1996) *Emotional intelligence: why it can matter more than IQ.* London: Bloomsbury Publishing.

29. Dweck, C. S. (2006) *Mindset how you can fulfil your potential.* New York: Ballantine Books.

30. Hellstedt, J.C. (1987) The coach/parent/athlete relationship. *The Sports Psychologist* 1, 151-160.

31. Pankhurst, A. (2014) *Natural talent only minor in elite athlete development research suggests.* University of Central Lancashire, accessed online at: http://www.uclan.ac.uk/news/natural_talent_minor_elite_athlete_develop ment_uclan_research.php

32. Smoll, F.L., Cumming, S.P., and Smith, R.E. (2011) Enhancing coach-parent relationships in youth sports: increasing harmony and minimizing hassle. *International Journal of Sports Science and Coaching*, 6(1), 13-25.

33. Cherry, K. (2014) *Instinct Theory of Motivation.* About Health, accessed online at: http://psychology.about.com/od/motivation/a/instinct-theory-of-motivation.htm

34. Bandura, A. (1977) *Social Learning Theory.* Upper Saddle River, NJ: Prentice-Hall.

35. Strudwick, T. In: Casteel, Q. (2015) *Manchester United's Tony Strudwick shares youth development philosophy.* Soccer Wire.com, accessed online at: http://www.soccerwire.com/blog-posts/manchester-uniteds-tony-strudwick-shares-youth-development-philosophy/

36. *Inside Out* (2015) Directed by Peter Docter. Burbank, CA: Walt Disney Studios Motion Pictures.

37. James, W. In: Munroe, M. (2005) *The Spirit of leadership*, p. 22. New Kensington, PA: Whitaker House.

38. Whitmore, J. (2009) *Coaching for Performance GROWing human potential and purpose: The principles and practices of coaching and leadership* (4ᵗʰ Ed.), p. 36, London: Nicholas Brealey Publishing.

39. *It's a wonderful life* (1946) Directed by Frank Capra. New York: RKO Radio Pictures.

40. Dickens, C. (1843) *A Christmas Carol*. London: Chapman & Hall.

41. Deci, E.L., and Ryan, R.M. (2004*) Handbook of self-determination research: Theoretical and applied issues*. Rochester, NY: University of Rochester Press.

42. Whitmore, J. (2009) *Coaching for Performance GROWing human potential and purpose: The principles and practices of coaching and leadership* (4ᵗʰ Ed.), p. 37, London: Nicholas Brealey Publishing.

43. Dickens, C. (1843) *A Christmas Carol*. London: Chapman & Hall.

44. Ashby, W. In: Bruce, G. (2010) *Personal and professional development*. Gíllí Bruce Training, accessed online at: http://www.gillibrucetraining.co.uk/personal.html

45. Mumford, E. (1988) *Ashby's Law of Requisite Variety and the design of expert systems.* Manchester: Manchester Business School.

46. Maslow, A.H. (2014) *Toward a psychology of being*. Bensenville, IL: Lushena Books.

47. Froch, C. (2011) *Carl Froch: The cobra, my story*, p. 103. London: Ebury Press.

48. Ericsson K. A., and Starkes J.L. (2003) *Expert Performance in Sports*. Champaign, Illinois: Human Kinetics.

49. Agassi, A. (2010) *Open*. London: HarperCollins.

50. Baker, J., Cobley, S., and Fraser-Thomas, J. (2009) What do we know about early sport specialization? Not much! *High Ability Studies*, 20, 77-89.

51. Kane, A. (2012) *A Race between Education and Catastrophe. High representative for disarmament affairs United Nations, p.1.* United Nations Office for Disarmament. The Global Forum on Disarmament and Non-Proliferation Education: Nagasaki, Japan. 10th August 2012.

52. Karnazes, D. (2006) *Ultramarathon man: Confessions of an all-night runner.* New York: Penguin.

53. Karnazes, D. In: Murphy, S. (2015) *Are we tabby cats trying to emulate cheetahs?* Runner's World Magazine, p.36, Plattsburgh, NY: Hearst Rodale Ltd.

54. Kington, M. In: McSmith, A. (2011) *Fond farewell to the genius of Miles Kington.* The Independent online, accessed online at: http://www.independent.co.uk/news/uk/this-britain/fond-farewell-to-the-genius-of-miles-kington-781024.html

55. Wilber, K. In: Visser, F. (2003*) Ken Wilber: Thought as passion*, p. 224. Albany, NY: State University of New York Press.

56. Gallwey, T. (1986) *The Inner game of tennis.* London: Macmillan Publishers.

57. Ibid

58. Pankhurst, A. (2014) *Natural talent only minor in elite athlete development research suggests.* University of Central Lancashire, accessed online at: http://www.uclan.ac.uk/news/natural_talent_minor_elite_athlete_development_uclan_research.php

59. Einstien, A. In: Mohama, B. (2013) *Intellectuals of café naderi*, p.67. Bloomington, IN: AuthorHouse.

60. Gladwell, M. (2005) *Blink: The power of thinking without thinking.* London: Penguin Books Ltd.

61. *The Wizard of Oz.* (1939) Directed by Victor Fleming. Beverly Hills, CA: Metro-Goldwyn-Mayer Studios, Inc.

62. Nater, S., and Gallimore, R. (2006) *You haven't taught until they have learned – John Wooden's principles*, p.122. West Virginia University Publishing, USA.

63. Gandhi, M. In: Morton, B. (2011) *Falser words were never spoken*. The New York Times, accessed online at: http://www.nytimes.com/2011/08/30/opinion/falser-words-were-never-spoken.html?_r=0

64. Johnson, M. (2012) *Gold Rush,* p.10. London: HarperSport Publishing.

65. Gunnell, S. In: Johnson, M. (2012) *Gold Rush,* p.263. London: HarperSport Publishing.

66. Jacobs, S. In: Williams, P., and Wimbish, D. (2006) *How to be like Coach Wooden: Life lessons from basketball's greatest leader*, p.252. Deerfield Beach, FL: Health Communications, Inc.

67. Wooden, J. (1997) Wooden – *A lifetime of observations and reflections on and off the court*, p.19. New York: McGraw-Hill Books.

68. Ovid (1556) *Metamorphoses (Books of transformations) VII. 20–21.* Joannes Gryphius.

69. Rock, D., and Page, L. (2009) *Coaching with the brain in mind*. New Jersey: John Wiley & Sons.

70. Spieth, J. In: Garside, K. (2015) *Spieth's sister inspires him*. IOL Sport, accessed online at: http://www.iol.co.za/sport/golf/spieth-s-sister-inspires-him-1.1844634#.VdtIy_lViko

71. Shinar, Y. (2007) *Think like a winner*. London: Vermillion Publishing, UK.

72. Nevill, D. In: Krieger, R.A. (2001) *Civilization's quotations: Life's ideal*, p.118. New York: Algora Publishing.

73. Ennis, J. (2013) *Unbelievable*, p.33. London: Hodder Paperbacks.

74. Lewis, T., Amini, F., and Lannon, R. (2001) *A general theory of love*. New York: Random House.

75. Roosevelt, T. In: Dorsey, T.J. (2013) *Point & figure charting the essential application for forecasting and trading market prices*, p.24. Hoboken, NJ: John Wiley & Sons, Inc.

76. *Inside Out* (2015) Directed by Peter Docter. Burbank, CA: Walt Disney Studios Motion Pictures.

77. Djokovic, N. (2014) *Serve to win: The 14-day gluten-free plan for physical and mental excellence*, p. 9. New York: Random House.

78. Nadal, R. (2012) *Rafa: My story*, p. 40. London: Sphere.

79. *The Karate Kid* (1984) Directed by John Avildsen. Los Angeles, CA: Columbia Pictures.

80. James, L. In: McMillen, M. (2014) *LeBron James pays homage to the mothers in his life.* WebMD, accessed online at: http://www.webmd.com/parenting/features/lebron-james-pays-homage-to-the-mothers-in-his-life

81. Peart, N. In: Lowrie-Chin, J. (2009) *Peart - the man who groomed Bolt.* Jamaica Observer column, accessed Online at: http://lowrie-chin.blogspot.co.uk/2009/08/peart-man-who-groomed-bolt.html

82. Aristotle (1999) *The Nicomachean Ethics – Translated by Terence Irwin.* Indianapolis, Indiana: Hackett Publishing.

83. Ashby, W.R. (1956): *An Introduction to Cybernetics*, London: Chapman & Hall.

84. Maslow, A. In: McRaney, D. (2012) *Maslow's Hammer are we entering a new phase in anthropology?* Psychology Today, accessed online at: https://www.psychologytoday.com/blog/you-are-not-so-smart/201203/maslows-hammer

85. Newton's first law (inertia) In: Grimshaw, P., Lees, A., Fowler, N., and Burden, A. (2006), *Sport and Exercise Biomechanics*, P.70, Abingdon: Taylor & Francis Group.

86. Murray, J. In: Price, A. (2015) *'It's like a heart attack' Judy Murray describes stress of watching Andy at Wimbledon.* Daily Express, accessed online at: http://www.express.co.uk/celebrity-news/589129/Judy-Murray-Andy-Murray-Wimbledon-stress-Good-Morning-Britain

87. Gibran, K. (1923) *The Prophet*, p.21. New York: Alfred. A. Knopf.

88. Frank, A. In: Hutchens, J. (2013) *The coaching calendar daily inspiration from the 'stress-less' coach*, p.298. Raleigh, NC: Lulu.

89. Tough, P. (2012) *How Children Succeed*. New York: Houghton Mifflin Harcourt Publishing Company.

90. Trenfor, A. In: Gow, B. (2014) *Showing you where to look, not what to see*. Teacher Magazine, accessed online at: https://www.teachermagazine.com.au/article/showing-you-where-to-look-not-what-to-see

91. 'Marginal gains philosophy' In: McClusky, M. (2014) *Faster, higher, stronger: The new science of creating superathletes, and how you can train like them*. New York: Plume.

92. Ferguson, A. (2015) *Leading*, p.44. London: Hodder & Stoughton.

93. Ibid, p.187.

94. African Proverb. In: Brady, A. (2011) *When all else fails...stAND*, p.69. Maitland, Florida: Xulon Press.

95. Federer, R. In: Eley, A. (2014) Roger Federer: I will not be a pushy parent. *BBC News*, accessed online at: http://www.bbc.com/news/world-30478486

96. Hadfield, C. (2013) *An astronaut's guide to life on earth*, p.159. London: Macmillan.

97. Ibid, p.163

98. Ibid, p.172

99. *Shawshank Redemption* (1994) Directed by Frank Darabont. Los Angeles, CA: Columbia Pictures.

Printed in Great Britain
by Amazon.co.uk, Ltd.,
Marston Gate.